THE CALL TO TEACHER LEADERSHIP

Sally J. Zepeda
R. Stewart Mayers
Brad N. Benson

EYE ON EDUCATION

6 DEPOT WAY WEST, SUITE 106

LARCHMONT, NY 10538

(914) 833–0551

(914) 833–0761 fax

www.eyeoneducation.com

Copyright © 2003 Eye On Education, Inc.

All Rights Reserved.

For information about permission to reproduce selections from this book, write: Eye On Education, Permissions Dept., Suite 106, 6 Depot Way West, Larchmont, NY 10538.

Library of Congress Cataloging-in-Publication Data

Zepeda, Sally J., 1956-
  The call to teacher leadership / Sally J. Zepeda, R. Stewart Mayers, Brad N. Benson.
    p. cm.
  Includes bibliographical references and index.
  ISBN 1-930556-50-0
  1. Teachers--Professional relationships--United States. 2. Teachers--In-service training--United states. 3. Educational leadership--United States. 4. Teacher participation in administration--United States. I. Mayers, R. Stewart, 1959- II. Benson, Brad N. III. Title.

LB1775.2 .Z47 2003
371.1'06--dc21

2002029752

10 9 8 7 6 5 4 3 2

Editorial and production services provided by
Richard H. Adin Freelance Editorial Services,
52 Oakwood Blvd., Poughkeepsie, NY 12603
(914-471-3566)

Also Available from EYE ON EDUCATION

**Instructional Supervision:
Applying Concepts and Tools**
Sally J. Zepeda

**Staff Development:
Practices That Promote Leadership in Learning Communities**
Sally J. Zepeda

Teacher Leader
Thomas S. Poetter and Bernard J. Badiali

**101 "Answers" for New Teachers and Their Mentors:
Effective Teaching Tips for Daily Classroom Use**
Annette L. Breaux

**Handbook on Teacher Portfolios for Evaluation
and Professional Development (Includes CD-ROM)**
Pamela Tucker, James Stronge, and Christopher Gareis

Coaching and Mentoring First-Year and Student Teachers
India J. Podsen and Vicki Denmark

**Teaching Matters:
Motivating & Inspiring Yourself**
Todd and Beth Whitaker

Dealing with Difficult Teachers, Second Edition
Todd Whitaker

Dealing with Difficult Parents
Todd Whitaker and Douglas Fiore

**Motivating And Inspiring Teachers:
The Educator's Guide For Building Staff Morale**
Todd Whitaker, Beth Whitaker, and Dale Lumpa

**Teacher Retention:
What Is Your Weakest Link?**
India J. Podsen

Data Analysis for Comprehensive Schoolwide Improvement
Victoria L. Bernhardt

TABLE OF CONTENTS

About the Authors xi
Case Study Contributors xiii
Acknowledgments xv
Introduction xvii

1 **Answering the Call to Teacher Leadership** 1
   Introducing Teacher Leadership 1
   The "Why" of Teacher Leadership 2
      The Need for Teacher Leaders 3
      Why Become a Teacher Leader? 5
   The "When" of Teacher Leadership 6
      Taking A.I.M. at Teacher Leadership 7
         Acumen 8
         Interest 8
         Motivation 8
      Responsibility to the Call to Teacher Leadership ... 9
   The "How" of Teacher Leadership 10
      Creating Opportunities for Leadership 10
      Reference Groups, Action Streams, and Teacher Leadership 12
   Teacher Leadership, Empowerment, and Voice 13
   The Formal and Informal Authority of Teacher Leaders ... 15
   New Work, New Responsibilities for Teacher Leaders ... 16
   Chapter Summary 19
   References 19

2 **The Thorny Issues of Teacher Leadership** 21
   Introducing Difficulties of Being a Teacher Leader ... 21
   Lines of Authority: Are Teacher Leaders Powerless Leaders? ... 22
      Reward Power 23
      Coercive Power 24
      Legitimate Power 24
      Expert Power 24
      Referent Power 25
      Informational Power 25
      Connection Power 26
      The "Magic" of Power 27
   Isolation 27
      Teacher Leaders as Trust-Builders 28

        Maintaining Open Communication 28
        Finding Time for Team Building 29
        Inducting New Members 30
    Isolation and Burnout 31
    Teacher Leaders and the Nature of Isolation 31
  Role Conflict and Role Ambiguity 32
    Time 32
    Relationships with Colleagues 33
    Managing Competing Site/District Demands 33
  Resolving Conflicts. 34
    Differentiation of Function among Parts of the Educational
        Organization 34
    Power Struggles between Persons and Subsystems 35
    Role Conflicts 35
    Differences in Interpersonal Style among Educators 36
    Stress Imposed on the Educational Organization by
        External Forces 37
  Teacher Leaders and Higher-Level Decision Making: Inclusion
    or Intrusion? 38
    Teacher Leaders and Higher-Level Decision Making 38
        The Inclusion of Teacher Leaders in Higher-Level
            Decision Making 38
        Intrusion into Higher-Level Decision Making:
            Working with Principals 39
  Chapter Summary 40
  References 41

3 Teacher Leadership in the Elementary School 43
  Introducing Teacher Leadership at the Elementary Level 43
  Partnerships with Parents 44
  Curriculum Alignment and Vertical Teaming 48
    Curriculum Analysis 48
    Curriculum Alignment 50
    Vertical Teaming 51
  The Work of Grade Level Leaders 53
  Coordinating the Work of Teachers across Grade Levels 55
    Monitoring Vertical Alignment of the Curriculum 55
    Maintaining Consistent Classroom Discipline Policies 56
  A Case Study from the Field: DeQueen Primary School,
    DeQueen, Arkansas 56
    Grade Level Leaders at DeQueen Primary School 57
    Smart Start Facilitators 57
    Cadre Persons and the Direct Instruction Coordinator 58
  The Work of a Teacher Facilitator 60
  The Unique Relationship between a Teacher Facilitator and
    the Principal 61

Table of Contents   vii

    A Case Study from the Field: Teacher Leadership at Gunter
        Elementary School, Gunter, Texas 61
        A Vision of Teacher Leadership. 62
        Teacher Leadership at Gunter Elementary 62
        The Teacher Facilitator at Gunter Elementary School 63
            The Teacher Facilitator as an Instructional Leader. 64
            The Teacher Facilitator as a Staff Developer 64
            Teacher Facilitator as Communicator. 65
        Teacher Leadership Creates Powerful Learning Opportunities for
            Teachers 65
    Chapter Summary 65
    References 66

4 Teacher Leadership in the Middle Grades 67
    Introducing Teacher Leadership in the Middle Grades 67
    The Instructional Lead Teacher (ILT) 68
    Getting Started as an Instructional Lead Teacher—Learning the Ropes . 70
        Network with Other ILTs in the District. 70
        Meet with the Team Leaders 70
        Provide Opportunities to Expand Interaction between and
            among Teams 72
    Credibility and Trust. 72
        Objectivity. 72
        Accountability, the Middle School Philosophy, and the Work
            of the Instructional Lead Teacher. 73
    A Case Study from the Field: School Governance and Teacher
         Leadership at Coile Middle School, Athens, Georgia 73
        Shared Decision Making. 74
        The School. 74
        Beginning Shared Governance 74
        Evaluation of Effectiveness 75
        Resources and Support 76
        Road Bumps 76
            Effective Teaming 77
            Clear and Thorough Communication 77
            The Impact of New Instructional Leaders 78
        Continual Evaluation 78
    Duties and Responsibilities of the Instructional Lead Teacher 79
        Development of Site Goals 79
        The Content of Middle School Professional Development 82
        Demonstration Lessons 82
        Working with Team Leaders: Promoting the Conditions that
            Foster Interdisciplinary Cooperation. 82
    The Middle School Team Leader 83
        What Do Team Leaders Do in the Middle School? 84
        Team Meetings 84

  Apples, Oranges, and Interdisciplinary Team Planning 86
Duties and Issues for the Team Leader 87
  Hiring New Staff Members 87
  The Transition to and from the Middle School 88
A Case Study from the Field: Camp Turning Points at Whittier Middle
  School, Norman, Oklahoma 89
  Camp Turning Points 89
  History 89
  The People 90
    The Coordinator 91
    Team Leaders 91
    National Guardsmen 91
    Parent Volunteers 91
  Action 91
  Evaluation 92
Transitioning from Middle School to High School 92
  Balancing the Core and Exploratory Programs 93
  Award Ceremonies and Guest Speakers 93
Chapter Summary 93
References 94

5 Teacher Leadership in the High School 95
Introducing Teacher Leadership in the High School 95
Perspectives about Teacher Leadership at the High School Level 96
The High School Department Chair 96
Getting Started 97
  Secure a Copy of the Job Description 97
  Review the Site Faculty Handbook 99
  Schedule a Meeting with the Administration 99
  Find a Mentor 100
The Work of Department Chairs 101
  Coordinating Activities for the Beginning and Ending of the
    School Year 101
  Managing the Department Budget 102
  Managing Facilities and Equipment 103
    Tracking Usage 104
    Maintaining the Department's Equipment 104
    Replacing Consumable Equipment 104
  Serving as a Content Specialist 105
  Conducting Department Meetings 105
    Tips for Running an Effective Department Meeting 106
  Developing Curriculum Guides 108
  Handling Student Placement Issues 109
    Sequential Courses 109
    Honors and Advanced Placement Classes 109
    Tryouts in the Fine Arts and Athletics 110

Table of Contents

Interviewing Teacher Candidates for the Department 110
    Interviewing Teaching Candidates 110
    Interviewing and the Law. 111
Writing Reports, Forecasting Needs: Profiling and Publicizing
    the Department's Accomplishments 112
    Communication that Informs 113
    Communication that Helps Plan 113
    Communication that Asks 113
    Communication that Evaluates 113
Balancing Departmental Work with the Duties of a Teacher. 114
A Case Study from the Field: TALENT—Teachers as Leaders:
    Encouraging New Thought—at Shiloh High School,
    Snellville, Georgia. 115
    TALENT—Teachers as Leaders: Encouraging New Thought—
        A Leadership Opportunity for Veteran Teachers 115
    TALENT 115
    What Does Teacher Leadership Mean for TALENT Teachers?. . . . 117
Chapter Summary. 117
References 118

6 Casting a Wide Net for Teacher Leadership 119
  A Call for Increased Leadership 119
  Scanning the Environment for Teacher Leadership Opportunities . . . 120
    Identify Leadership Opportunities 120
    Cast a Wide Net. 121
  Teacher Leadership Is Invitational 122
    Provide Professional Development and Mentoring for Teacher
        Leaders. 123
    Assuming Leadership Can Be Risky Business for the Newcomer
        to Leadership 124
  An Extended Case Study from the Field—Gwinnett County Public
    Schools, Georgia. 124
    Philosophy of Teacher Leadership 125
    Teachers as Leaders, Inc. (TAL) 125
    Early Beginnings of TAL 126
    TAL Today. 127
    The Philosophy of TAL. 128
        The Goals of TAL 128
    The Leadership Curriculum of TAL. 129
    Program Evaluation 130
    Lessons Learned. 130
    Funding TAL 131
    Networking 131
    Benefits of TAL 132
    Administrative Support Needed to Promote Teacher Leadership. . 134
        Principals 134

  District Level 135
  Community Level. 136
  The Heart of Teacher Leadership 136
 References 137

Subject and Author Index 139

About the Authors

Dr. Sally J. Zepeda is a former high school teacher, director of special programs, assistant principal, and principal. Her books include: *Instructional Supervision: Applying Tools and Concepts; Staff Development: Practices that Promote Leadership in Learning Communities; Special Programs in Regular Schools: Historical Foundations, Standards, and Contemporary Issues* (with Michael Langenbach); *The Reflective Supervisor: A Practical Guide for Educators* (with Raymond Calabrese); and *Supervision and Staff Development in the Block* (with Stewart Mayers). Sally is an associate professor and the Graduate Coordinator of the Educational Leadership Program at the University of Georgia.

Dr. R. Stewart Mayers is a former classroom teacher, department chair, and district staff developer. He has taught mathematics (middle school through Advanced Placement Calculus), history, and German in both traditional and block schedules. Stewart is an assistant professor of Educational Instruction and Leadership at Southeastern Oklahoma State University, and he is coauthor (with Sally Zepeda) of *Supervision and Staff Development in the Block.*

Dr. Brad N. Benson is the Director of Fine Arts for the Norman, Oklahoma Public Schools. He is a former elementary, middle, and high school instrumental music teacher. Brad has 16 years experience as a department chair—10 years at the high-school level and six years at the middle school level.

Case Study Contributors

Lynda Beltrani, Principal
DeQueen Primary School
Treating Plant Road
DeQueen, AR 71832
(870) 642-3100
Fax: 870-642-7360
Online: www.leopards.k12.ar.us
DeQueen Public Schools
Mr. Bill Blackwood, Superintendent

Cheyrl A. Cohagan, Principal
Gunter Elementary School
Dara Arrington, Teacher Facilitator
100 W. Pecan
Gunter, TX 75058
903-433-5315
Fax: (903) 433-1184
Online: www.gunterisd.org
Gunter Independent School District
Mr. Richard W. Cohagan,
Superintendent

Yvonne Frey, Principal
Head Elementary School
1801 Hewatt Rd.
Lilburn, GA 30047
(770) 972-8050
Fax: (770) 736-4498
Online: www.headelementary.org
Gwinnett County Public Schools
Mr. J. Alvin Wilbanks, Superintendent

Dr. Patty Heitmuller, Principal
Harbins Elementary School
3550 New Hope Road
Dacula, GA 30019
(770) 682-4270
Fax: (770) 682-4285
Online: harbins.home.mindspring.com
Gwinnett County Public Schools
Mr. J. Alvin Wilbanks, Superintendent

Dr. Gale Hulme, Program Director
Georgia's Leadership Institute for
School Improvement
866 W. Peachtree Street, NW
Atlanta, GA 30308
(404) 385-4088
FAX: (404) 894-9675
gale.hulme@galeaders.org

Tim Jarboe, Principal
W. R. Coile Middle School
110 Old Elberton Road
Winterville, GA 30601
(706) 357-5318
Fax: (706) 357-5321
Online: www.clarke.k12.ga.us/coile
Clarke County School District
Dr. Lewis Holloway, Superintendent

Dr. Lea Arnau, Director of Staff Development, Gwinnett County Public Schools
Dr. James Kahrs, Principal
Shiloh High School
4210 Shiloh Road
Snellville, GA 30039
(770) 972-8471
Fax: (770) 736-4345
Online: www.shilohhighschool.org
Gwinnett County Public Schools
Mr. J. Alvin Wilbanks, Superintendent

Billy Nettles, Principal
Whittier Middle School
2000 West Brooks
Norman, OK 73069
(405) 366-5956
Fax: (405) 447-6562
Online: www.norman.k12.ok.us
Norman Public Schools
Dr. Joseph Siano, Superintendent

Vivian Stranahan, Principal
Shiloh Elementary School
2400 Ross Road
Snellville, GA 30039
(770) 985-6883
Fax: (770) 736-2061
Online: www.gwinnett.k12.ga.us/ShilohES
Gwinnett County Public Schools
Mr. J. Alvin Wilbanks, Superintendent

Acknowledgments

It takes more than just authors to write a book, and it is no different with this book. We thank the case study contributors, who are listed in the text of the book, and in the Case Study Contributors listing, along with their contact information. We thank Dr. Gale Hulme, Program Director for Georgia's Leadership Institute for School Improvement, for the insights she provided about teacher leadership during the process of writing this book. As the former Executive Director of Professional Development for Gwinnett County Public Schools (GA), she coordinated the writing of the TAL, Inc. Case Study with her colleagues in Gwinnett County. In addition, we thank Michael Mattingly, Executive Director of Elementary Operations, Houston County, Georgia Public Schools; and Dr. Charlotte King Eady, Director of the Opportunity Academy, a Charter School of the Griffin-Spalding, Georgia Public Schools. Ms. Leslee Cunningham, Hill Country Middle School, Eanes School District, Austin, Texas, provided numerous insights into teacher leadership in the middle grades.

We were fortunate to have external reviewers provide the benefit of their experiences as teacher leaders and the wisdom they gained from working with teacher leaders:

Claudia Geocaris, Principal, Hinsdale South High School, Darien, IL

Douglas B. Hartman, Director of Human Resources, Douglas County Schools, Castle Rock, CO

Pat Michael, Director, Elementary Education and Professional Development, Ridgefield Public Schools, CT

Keith Nomura, Principal, Lincoln Middle School, Alameda, CA

To the high school department chairs, middle school team leaders, elementary lead teachers, and grade-level leaders who have opened their worlds to us along the way, we are grateful. These professionals welcomed us into their schools to watch teacher leaders in action.

We appreciate the work ethic of Ms. Teresa Gidden, secretary for the Department of Educational Instruction and Leadership at Southeastern Oklahoma State University. We would not have met our deadline without her countless hours of typing changes in, and formatting, this manuscript.

And to Bob Sickles, who had the vision for the need to explore teacher leadership not only as a calling but as a way to explore the complexities of the work of teacher leaders. He lit the torch.

Introduction

Teachers are leaders by the very nature of the work they do in schools. Some of the work of teacher leaders is bundled in formal positions; however, much of the work of teacher leaders is more informal. This book examines the work of teacher leaders across K–12 schools and includes an examination of formal roles such as the lead teacher, grade-level coordinator, and department chair. One of the features of this book is that it examines not only the work of teacher leaders, but it also examines the formal and informal leadership that these leaders exert to create leadership in others—fellow teachers.

This book is a resource to help teacher leaders fine-tune skills needed to lead while they accomplish the work of teacher leadership. Gaining confidence as a leader occurs, in part, with understanding the complexities of teacher leadership—conflict, role identity, and risk taking, while at the same time getting "things done" at the school.

Teacher leaders exert their influence beyond the school as well because they serve on both school and system-wide committees, they become active in professional organizations, and they share their expertise with others. Teacher leaders inspire by sharing leadership opportunities with others, and this is the heart and soul of teacher leaders. In Chapter 1, we lead teachers through the process of reflecting on the call to teacher leadership, and, in Chapter 2, we discuss the thorny issues of teacher leadership so that the teacher leader is in a good position to avoid some of the traps that can occur while being a leader.

Chapters 3, 4, and 5 include in-depth discussions of the work of teacher leaders at the elementary, middle, and high school levels. Particular attention to grade-specific work across the K–12 spectrum serves to ground our discussions on teacher leadership not only for those in formal positions, but also for all teachers who engage in leadership at these levels. In Chapter 6, we "tie together" all the pieces of teacher leadership, regardless of grade level, position, or title, and we conclude with a comprehensive case study of one school system's success in "casting a wide net"—in capturing the leadership of hundreds of teachers since its inception. In each chapter, we offer not only the tools of leadership but also snapshots of teacher leadership in a variety of settings—urban, rural, and suburban—as a way to bring to light the powerful impact that teacher leaders can have in schools and the many lives they touch—those of teachers, students, administrators, and parents, to name a few.

1
Answering the Call to Teacher Leadership

In this Chapter
- The "Why" of Teacher Leadership
- The "When" of Teacher Leadership
- The "How" of Teacher Leadership
- Teacher Leadership, Empowerment, and Voice
- The Formal and Informal Authority of Teacher Leaders
- New Work, New Responsibilities for Teacher Leaders

Introducing Teacher Leadership

Teachers are leaders, and common sense tells us that they are the most valuable resource in any school system. In their classrooms, teachers lead students—guiding instruction, managing the classroom environment, and juggling daily the responsibilities of working with other teachers, parents, and administrators. Formal leadership positions often take teachers out of the classroom and into an administrative office. Teachers face a dilemma because, for many, the only way to become a leader is to either opt out of the classroom for a full-time administrative position or to teach part-time while assuming the responsibility of instructional coordinator, lead teacher, or department chair. While fulfilling these part-time positions, teacher leaders are often caught with "one foot in and one foot out" of teaching.

This book presents the premise that teachers can be leaders in their schools and school systems without necessarily having to opt out of the classroom full-time. The construct of teacher leadership is not a new one, but one that is becoming increasingly important across all levels—elementary, middle, and high school. All teachers have the capacity to be leaders, but the development of leadership needs to be promoted from within the rank and file of teachers. Leadership needs to be supported by the systems in which teachers work, and teachers who assume leadership roles—both formal and informal ones—need to be nurtured. The work that Teacher Leaders do can have a profound effect on student learning, school improvement, and the overall ability of the school to build capacity for ongoing learning and development.

This chapter explores the "why," "when," and "how" of teacher leadership. The formal and informal roles that teacher leaders assume are examined, leading logically to the work that teacher leaders do. From such an exploration, teachers may be in a better position to understand the complexities of the work of teacher leaders—nurturing colleagues, supporting the instructional program, and making decisions that affect both students and adults—as they assume leadership roles and positions across K–12 schools.

The "Why" of Teacher Leadership

Why do teachers enter the profession? Teachers have an altruistic calling to the profession, and they *want* to make a difference in the lives of the children they teach. Why become a teacher leader? Teachers become leaders because they *can* make a difference. Teacher leaders answer the call because they want to make a difference—with other teachers, the school, the district, and, ultimately, with students. Teacher leadership is a calling to a higher level of service. Teacher leaders have the courage to "step up to the plate," and they assume incredible responsibilities that often:

- Go beyond the contract day.
- Fall outside the sphere of monetary compensation.
- Place them at odds with bargaining units.
- Create tensions among fellow faculty and administrators because they take a stand, they involve themselves wholeheartedly in their work as teacher leaders, and they seek change.

Yet, teacher leaders still press on to take a lead in the work that goes beyond the classroom. Teacher leaders are interested in change, and Méndez-Morse (1992) cites Nickse (1977), who found that teachers as change agents emerge because:

- *teachers have a vested interest*, "they care about what they do and how they do it and feel a sense of responsibility for their efforts;"
- *teachers have a sense of history*, they are "aware of the norms of their colleagues;"
- *teachers know the community*, and "have information concerning the values and attitudes of the community" and

- *teachers can implement change,* they "are where the action is ... in the position to initiate planned change on the basis of need." (p. 19)

And although there is more than compelling research and perspective on the positive effects of teacher leadership (Lambert, 1998), leadership from within the rank and file of teachers has been slow to evolve in our schools for a variety of reasons—lack of time, overbooked schedules, outside commitments, and administrators who do not wish to have teachers leading. Often, teacher leadership rests in coveted positions—lead teachers, department chairs, and instructional coordinators. These formal positions are important but so are the informal leadership roles, duties, and responsibilities that teacher leaders without formal title assume. Although this book examines teacher leadership from the perspectives of the teachers who assume more formal leadership roles, we believe that teacher leaders emerge through the work they do as:

- Presenters at workshops (at the site, district, and beyond).
- Members of curriculum committees that make instructional decisions.
- Mentors and peer coaches.
- Team leaders for grade and subject areas.
- Speakers at parent, board, and community meetings.
- Cooperating teachers.
- Faculty representatives on visiting accreditation teams.
- Members on school improvement teams.
- Members of faculty and administrative search committees.

Whereas one teacher leader can have an impact, a cadre of teacher leaders within schools and districts can effect change and improvement not only in the systems in which they serve but also in the lives of the people who live and breathe life into schools. Teacher leaders can influence the environment—student and adult learning and morale—in powerful, positive, and pervasive ways. Teacher leaders provide the impetus for change and innovation. This is the why of teacher leadership.

The Need for Teacher Leaders

The development of teacher leadership in schools and districts is a priority for a variety of important reasons, and there is a pressing need for teacher leaders to assume leadership responsibilities both at the site as well as at the district levels. The success of school systems depends on strong teacher leadership. Faced with increasing pressures and time demands through state and federal regulations, testing programs, and frequent policy changes, administrators rely on teachers from within their buildings to assume some of the leadership roles and tasks ordinarily carried out by administrative leaders.

Teacher leaders have expertise, and they often want to further develop this expertise through expanding their involvement in the work of schools beyond the classroom. Central-office administrators also find themselves increasingly mired in translating federal programs and aligning curriculum to meet the needs for state and national assessments, and, as a result of this focus, they rely on teacher leaders to assist, coordinate, and deliver programs at the site level.

Teacher leaders are able to provide the "big picture" view of the educational system in which they work. Without leadership from teachers, an important part of processes, policies, and practices is missing. Another "big picture" issue that teacher leaders address is the "shared vision" of the site and district. Well-informed administrators are aware that to spread the organization's vision, teacher leaders are the carriers of the message. Teachers not only carry the message, but they also infuse the energy to bring the vision to fruition. Just as students often communicate with more clarity and meaning to other students, teacher leaders can do the same with other teachers.

Teacher leaders are a source of valid information within a school or district. Teacher leaders understand the communication networks, and they know how to get the word out to the troops. Teacher leaders understand the patterns of communication, the culture of the school, and they know how to effectively communicate within the context of the school. With regard to the most practical matters and to plan for the future, realistic and grounded information provided through a teacher leader will be invaluable for progress in schools interested in school improvement.

A teacher leader is one who informs, who actively gathers information from colleagues and, more to the point of leadership, will deliver that information in a manner suitable to the person and situation regardless of the risks. Teacher leaders are, by virtue of the position they occupy in school systems, willing to assume an element of risk. Teacher leaders are risk takers.

Schools need teacher leaders, and teacher leaders are present in our schools—from the novice to the most seasoned veteran. Further, the opportunity to lead is a fundamental right and responsibility of everyone who enters the teaching profession. Without avenues for teacher leadership, we risk losing the backbone of our schools—teachers who are the schools' most valuable resource. Involvement in leadership activities and positions may be an excellent remedy for the burnout some of our best and brightest teachers suffer because they lack opportunities to learn, grow, and share with others. Teacher leadership can offer those creative and highly motivated teachers a path of expression and action that will not only make a difference with others, but also will help to renew and reinvigorate them.

Why Become a Teacher Leader?

Why should a teacher become a leader? The answer, in general, is probably twofold—for others and for yourself. When you carry out effective leadership as a teacher, you are contributing not only to the educational organization, but also, even more importantly, to the people who are a part of the system. Through leadership, you have a chance to give of yourself to your profession and to make full use of the talents, abilities, and training that the process of education most likely helped you develop, both as a student and as a professional. You will be able to see some results almost immediately, whereas other dividends will be longer in coming and may even go unrecognized. Regardless of the immediacy of the outcomes, a teacher leader has a chance to help others grow—students, teachers, administrators, parents, and the community. The opportunity to foster growth will yield the same, if not a greater, sense of fulfillment that teachers derive from the classroom.

A part of the reason to become a teacher leader involves rewards. Some teacher leaders may at first be hard put to express the rewards that leadership brings them, but on reflection, they find their work to be highly rewarding both intrinsically and extrinsically. Imagine the good feeling you will have when, as a leader, you begin to think in terms of the "big picture;" when you no longer suffer from the insular shortsightedness that can occur by "hiding in the classroom." When you free yourself, you also help to free other teachers and even administrators from the "educational myopia" that can cause stagnation in the very best of schools and districts. Teacher leadership can foster an intense sense of self-satisfaction and increased self-worth. As adults move through stages of development, they have a desire to give back to the profession, to make a difference, and to make their mark professionally and personally.

Picture yourself increasing the scope of your influence. You still have the student–teacher relationship, but through teacher leadership, you can influence other teachers, policies, hiring, and budget—the list continues. Through these activities, you can have a positive effect on more than the students in your classroom. You will be able to envision new ideas, new methods, new structures, and new ways of doing things and have a means to see your vision and plan to fruition. The excitement of seeing what you have imagined, planned, and prepared for become reality is actually a large part of the reward for any creative process. Teacher leadership can offer the teacher a means to exercise more creativity, and, with the real possibility of results, derive a sense of fulfillment.

A reward that is sorely lacking in the area of teacher leadership is money, and much more emphasis needs to be placed on affirming the value of teacher leaders through salary adjustments or stipends. Although a teacher or teacher leader rarely, if ever, does "what is good" and "what is right" for the money, the respect and value that monetary rewards offer can go a long way to bolster both the individual teacher leader and the cause of teacher leaders.

Teacher leaders are self-directed. Leadership roles and tasks give teacher leaders an outlet for their energies and ideas as well as a means to channel their work toward a cause greater than that of any one individual. Another reason to become a teacher leader is its by-product—that of learning to be a leader and the process one goes through in becoming a leader. Almost without exception, teachers who become involved in leadership activities become better teachers. The new experiences, professional development, viewpoints, and ideas all seem to lend themselves to growth in the classroom. The stimulating atmosphere of teacher leadership creates a new relationship with students and, usually, a more mutually beneficial relationship with colleagues, administrators, parents, and the community. If this were the only reward of teacher leadership, the journey would be well worth it.

As a teacher leader, you are in a unique position to offer your bank of experience and expertise to others. As a teacher, you have your feet firmly placed on the ground, and as a teacher leader, you can reach for the sky. These are a few reasons *why* a teacher should become a teacher leader, but are there any clues as to *when* a teacher might be ready to consider starting down the road of teacher leadership?

The "When" of Teacher Leadership

How is one to know when to consider becoming a teacher leader? There are probably many clues and signs of a teacher's readiness for teacher leadership. It is important to realize that some of the clues will come from within the teacher, but some will also come from people and situations outside of the teacher. One of the ways to discern a readiness for teacher leadership is that your antennae are tuned in to those very clues.

You might be ready to become a teacher leader if:

- You have developed a sense of "perspective" about your teaching, the school climate, and the district organization.
- You come up with plans in your mind that might be an improvement on the ones in place or those in preparation.
- You have something of value (skills, information, abilities) that you know you can offer other teachers, administrators, and the district.

- You find yourself speaking up at faculty meetings and professional development sessions, and your thoughts receive favorable responses from presenters and other faculty.
- You notice that other teachers often solicit your opinions and advice.
- You find that teachers or administrators increasingly rely on you to organize and lead various activities.
- You are "volunteered" by other teachers for leadership roles and tasks.
- Administrators seek your help and advice on various school matters, and, even more importantly, they return to you for more help and advice.
- You find that the faculty and the administration trust you, and they have confidence in you.
- You have an aching desire to help direct the flow of teaching and learning through a wider sphere of personal influence.
- You have hunches and take risks based on those hunches.
- You have the confidence to disagree with the status quo and to act on your convictions.
- You are willing to take on more responsibility and actively seek it out.

Teacher leadership is not dependent on years of experience, and teachers can emerge as leaders across the career continuum. Beginning teachers have specialized training marked by recency, and they can help to inform practice. Veteran teachers have the knowledge, skills, and expertise developed over time, and their wisdom can help inform practice.

Taking A.I.M. at Teacher Leadership

With these leadership clues recognized and acknowledged, the potential teacher leader can take an inventory for readiness. Leadership at any level is a responsibility and contains the seeds for both frustration and joy. Knowing that you are ready to become a teacher leader will not only support the confidence others have in you, but will also help you to develop the self-assurance needed for the leadership journey. However, it is important to remember that teachers who aspire to be leaders need training and mentoring to work as successfully with colleagues as they have with students.

Acumen

Some teachers, it may seem, are born leaders, whereas others may develop into leaders. In either case, a teacher must have a "feel" for leadership, an almost innate understanding of at least some of the underlying skills and tools necessary for leadership. They are typically adept at interpersonal relationships, are "likable," but also act from principle rather than a need to be liked. They seem to excel at codifying, organizing, and planning—at bringing new thoughts and concepts to others in an approachable way.

One way to determine your acumen for leadership is to find a current leader that you and others hold in high esteem and *ask* that person if you have the beginnings of what it takes to be a leader. Another reliable method for determining adeptness for leadership is to take measure of previous leadership activities that you have had an opportunity to assume, and ask: Did others follow? What was the outcome of your leadership? Did the "followers" respond to you? Answering these questions honestly will go a long way in helping you determine if you have acumen for teacher leadership.

Interest

A genuine interest in leadership and in leading is a necessary ingredient for success as a teacher leader. You may wonder what it would be like to be the leader, what it would feel like, and what action you would take. A potential teacher leader will most likely closely observe other leaders with particular attention to the results obtained, the method through which they are attained, and the feelings and reactions of others involved (including those of the potential leader). Teachers who have an interest in formalizing leadership engage in a variety of activities to help prepare them for the work of leadership. Teacher leaders research the literature, read books, ask questions of leaders both within and outside of the school district, and attend workshops and seminars. An active interest in leadership can do more than lead teachers to leadership positions; it can also help support the continuous growth in which the successful teacher leader engages as part of the process of emerging as a leader.

Motivation

A future teacher leader must have a strong sense of motivation for becoming a leader. Your resolve and sense of purpose will be evident to those you lead and will be highly important to the degree of success you achieve as a teacher leader. As previously stated, a teacher leader's motivation might include helping others—this may be your "mission." Your motivation might also rest in a desire to see that the best things are done on behalf of students. Your motivation may stem from a personal commitment to education that you can realize through exercising leadership.

In all probability, others will not appreciate selfishness; however, there should be personal elements in your motivation toward becoming a teacher leader. Positive feelings, an increased sense of worth, and an enhancement of your professional life may all motivate you toward teacher leadership. Determining your motivation is largely an introspective process, but you can glean information from your interactions with others.

Another common motivation may be that of "advancing" your career. Teacher leadership may lead to several forms of leadership roles while the teacher is still in the classroom. Assuming these roles and the responsibilities that accompany them may serve to satisfy many teachers, but success in the teacher leader position can also lead to leadership positions out of the classroom. Depending on skills and abilities, teacher leaders may be approached to become assistant principals, curriculum directors, or "managing" directors. Success in these positions may lead to leadership as a principal, assistant superintendent, or superintendent, or to positions with state departments or national associations. The leadership career path can take many different avenues once you have started on the journey. Motivation is a key to developing and to sustaining a successful career in all leadership arenas.

Responsibility to the Call to Teacher Leadership

Teacher leaders feel compelling reasons for responding to the call to leadership. Although the "why" of teacher leaders provides pervasive reasons for teachers to respond to this call, equally pressing is the question, "Who will lead our schools if teachers do not respond to the call to leadership?" The web site for the UCLA School Management Program Academies (http://www.smp.gseis.ucla.edu/smp/programs/ILA/leadership.html) reports:

> There have been many questions raised regarding how the schools of the future are going to be led. From site-based decision making to active participation in decisions, teachers are being asked to be leaders in their schools. Others have looked at developing a leaderless organization. Perhaps a better way of looking at leadership in schools is to consider how to develop a leaderful organization, a place where leadership permeates every part of the entire structure of the organization....We see teacher leaders as individuals who:
>
> ♦ Practice democratic collaboration;
>
> ♦ Show bold, socially responsible leadership;
>
> ♦ Focus on continuous improvement;

- Are consistently aware of equity, access and inclusion;
- Have high ethical standards in their professional roles;
- Are reflective and thoughtful.

These are the qualities of teacher leaders.

The "How" of Teacher Leadership

Knowing that teacher leadership is sorely needed in schools, it remains for us to explore how to become a teacher leader. The *how* of teacher leadership requires creativity, perseverance, and preparation. Perhaps the first and best step is to be an exemplary teacher. If colleagues and administrators respect your teaching skills, you will have a much better chance of finding, or being offered, opportunities for leadership. The future teacher leader must also be aware of her/his environment. Know how things work and who works them. Be familiar with decision-making processes, how decisions are delivered and acted on, and by whom. It is also requisite for teacher leaders to know their teaching colleagues. Teacher leaders are aware of their colleagues' strengths, interests, and styles of learning, and understand how colleagues relate to others in the school.

To understand the big picture of the school system, the teacher leader needs to be familiar with the shared vision of the district and the site. Also, familiarity and understanding of district goals, school site plans, district and site committees, action plans, and the needs of the school are essential to the success of a teacher leader. You can prepare to assume leadership roles by finding a trusted mentor, another teacher, or administrator with whom to discuss opportunities for leadership. You can also read as much of the literature on leadership as possible, and even explore leadership in other professions for alternative points of view. Another precursor to teacher leadership is involvement in professional development activities and programs that deal with leadership development. In Chapter 6, the Teachers as Leaders (TAL, Inc.) initiative in Gwinnett County provides a comprehensive view of teacher leadership across a school district.

Creating Opportunities for Leadership

Rather than being a passive prospect for teacher leadership, you can actively take steps to enhance and create the opportunity for leading. Seek out and volunteer for leadership or administrative tasks, no matter how small or short-lived they may be. A willingness to assume leadership sends a signal to administrators and teachers that you are interested and motivated to be a teacher leader. Begin by asking for leadership responsibilities, then prove yourself, and then ask for more. For the teacher leader, any leadership role or position will most likely be the result of "earned leadership." Developing a record of effectiveness and trust is important in the process of becoming a teacher leader.

A strategy for creating a leadership niche is similar to "looking for gaps" to fill. With your knowledge of the district and the site, the administration, faculty, and students, begin to observe those processes within the school that need attention. The future teacher leader makes a "needs assessment for teacher leadership" in his/her school and district. Once you have identified these needs, do the research and the legwork, and develop a plan to address the needs using your skills and abilities as part of the solution. Presenting a plan to administrators with a workable solution will also serve you in your future leadership endeavors.

Teacher leaders have skills that are indicative of leadership. Teacher leaders have the ability to be instructional leaders, and they can:

- Provide demonstration lessons and share their skills with others.
- Develop and consistently use lines of communication with teachers and administrators.
- Provide assessments for content, delivery, and instruction while serving as a peer coach or mentor.
- Have a view of the "big picture" for decisions that are made at the site and district level.
- Offer input on site and district goals and plans.
- Develop professional growth plans and have them evaluated by peers and administrators.
- Attend and take an active part in staff meetings.
- Support students, faculty, staff, and administration with time and talent.
- Engage in peer coaching or action research projects.
- Individually, or collaboratively, mentor new teachers.
- Take an active role in evaluating and developing curriculum.
- Attend out-of-school events and performances in both an official and an unofficial capacity.
- Demonstrate through teaching and through communication with others the value and application of professional development information and activities.

Reference Groups, Action Streams, and Teacher Leadership

One of the challenges of becoming a teacher leader involves developing the capacity to hold several points of view at the same time. A reference group holds a particular viewpoint and often shares a way of thinking and acting particular to that group. The two main reference groups to which a future teacher leader must relate are teachers and administrators. Teacher reference groups are complex. The teacher leader must not exclusively rely on self/teacher perceptions, but must expand this view to include "other" teachers. Teacher reference groups might include various grade levels or content areas and may change in each leadership situation. The key for the teacher leader is to recognize this fact and to grasp the viewpoint of several groups in the school.

Understanding the administrative reference group may be more difficult for a teacher. Discussions with an open and trusted administrator will certainly help, as will reading literature directly related to leadership. The teacher should take advantage of every opportunity to "be around" and to observe administrators, paying particular attention to lines of thought and items deemed to be important.

How to be a teacher leader, therefore, assumes that the teacher can think like an administrator and a teacher, or, at least, hold both points of view while making plans or decisions. This "dual vision" may enable the teacher leader to see things in a different way. In fact, the teacher leader may be able to discern patterns or processes in the school environment that would not be apparent to separate reference groups. By understanding elements of both reference groups, the teacher leader will be able to move with confidence and trust among and between groups.

A teacher cannot become a teacher leader without becoming a part of the decision-making process and leadership action in the school or district. Leadership decisions and actions occur in schools on a daily basis and across several levels. Each decision and accompanying action becomes a part of the decisions and actions that follow. There is a flow of action in the school. This action stream is the vehicle through which the teacher can become a leader.

Identifying the source or sources of the action stream is the first step in the "how" of becoming an active leader. Once made, the teacher prepares for leadership by establishing contact with a source. Preparing and positioning are essential elements in this process whether the teacher sticks in a toe or dives head first into the stream. Teacher leaders can make a difference because even a small change in the current can alter the direction of the stream.

After the teacher takes the leadership plunge, the teacher and the administrator will understand the impact of teacher leadership on the direction of the stream. The stream may branch into new and innovative directions, or it may widen to include more decision makers. The leadership action stream is the lifeblood of the institution, and teacher leaders can play a very important role. In fact, with numerous teacher leaders in action, the stream may develop rivulets or capillaries that may oxygenate, vitalize, and nourish all aspects of an educational organism. Now that the teacher leader has become a part of the action, we need to learn more about teacher leadership—what it requires and what is needed for success.

Teacher Leadership, Empowerment, and Voice

Teacher leadership is more than teachers assuming "add-on" responsibilities such as serving on before- and after-school committees, attending a meeting on behalf of an administrator, compiling data for an accreditation report, or assuming an additional duty or teaching assignment; nevertheless, teacher leaders could very well be engaged in these types of activities.

It is not what teachers do *per se* that makes them teacher leaders. Teacher leadership is much more than that. Teachers are leaders when they act and respond with authority and make decisions that are supported. Teachers want, and need, opportunities to enlarge their sphere of influence beyond the confines of the classroom without necessarily leaving teaching for a formal administrative position. When teachers can act with this type of authority, they are empowered because their "voices" are being acknowledged and, more importantly, *heard*.

Teachers who are empowered have voice, and through the process of becoming empowered, teachers develop what Romanish (1991) terms an "authentic voice." Empowerment and voice are more than having a mere "say" or "vote" on an issue, and, Romanish asserts, "having a vote is not the equivalent of having a voice because those with a genuine voice have a say in what choices are offered for the vote" (p. 59).

Lightfoot (1986) indicates that, "Empowerment refers to the opportunities a person has for autonomy, responsibility, choice, and authority" (p. 9), and it is the authority exerted that makes a teacher a leader. The empowering qualities of voice as envisioned by Jalongo (1991) are detailed in Figure 1.1. Voice is an essential precursor for teacher leadership and it signals empowerment.

Figure 1.1. Teacher Voice Leads to Empowerment

Qualities of Teacher Voice

Voice allows teachers to be heard..............

Voice has a vocal range........................

Voice can be extended through practice.........

Voice is developmental........................ Leads to

Voice resides within the individual..............

Voice is a combination of talent, confidence, experience, and persistence...................

→ EMPOWERMENT

Teachers are leaders when they are empowered by the system and its people. Teacher leadership is more easily understood, perhaps, by examining first why teacher leadership has been slow to evolve. According to Troen and Boles (1994):

> Teaching is not a profession that values or encourages leadership within its ranks. The hierarchical nature of public schools is based on the 19th century model, with the consequent adversarial relationship of administration as management and teachers as labor. Like factory workers in the 1800s, teachers all have equal status. Leadership opportunities are extremely limited. (p. 275)

The hierarchical model of leadership in schools is slowly giving way to the development of formal and informal leadership structures with teachers assuming more responsibility for their work and the overall operations of the school that have, in the past, solely rested within the duty of the school's administration.

Teacher "leadership is iterative," and teachers, given the opportunity, will provide the energy for leadership to be multiplied (Lieberman & Miller, 1999, p. 22). Regardless of what teacher leaders do or the roles they assume, leadership is needed from *within* the organization. The ways in which teachers assume leadership will be a function of the context of the school, the history of teacher leadership in the school, the relationships and communication patterns between teachers and administrators, and a host of other variables that are unique to each school site. How teachers exert leadership will depend very much on these context variables, and equally, on how principals promote the empowerment of their teachers.

Principals can recognize and acknowledge the competence that teachers bring to the learning environment, resulting in teachers who are empowered to assume their professional right to leadership. It is this recognition and acknowledgment that signals that principals believe in, and have confidence in, teachers and their ability to self-determine and self-direct the formal and informal leadership that they assume.

The Formal and Informal Authority of Teacher Leaders

Although *formal* leadership roles are limited by the size and composition of the school and are relegated primarily through the positional power of an office (principal, assistant principal), there are other formal leadership positions for teachers to assume, such as instructional lead teacher, instructional coordinator, grade level leader, and department chair. Although these teacher leadership positions are formal, there are other ways that teachers provide formal leadership without a title (e.g., mentor, committee member). Teachers exercise formal leadership when they engage in such work as being a mentor for a first-year teacher, earning an advanced degree, serving on a teacher- or principal-selection committee, formally presenting at local, state, and national conferences, or writing an article for a professional journal. However, many of the traditional endeavors where teachers have found opportunities to demonstrate leadership abilities fall at the secondary level.

However, opportunities for teachers to assume *informal* leadership abound in the schools and systems in which they work. Informally, teachers exert leadership when they review textbooks and other materials during the textbook adoption process, engage in staff development and other learning opportunities, such as attending graduate school, or participating in civic events within the larger community. Sometimes, teacher leaders engage in both informal and formal leadership activities, especially when they serve as role models in the communities in which their schools are situated. Teacher leadership can exist both formally and informally in any school. Teacher leadership, albeit formal or informal, "consists of two issues (a) enabling experiences provided within an organization that foster autonomy, choice, and responsibility; and (b) allowing the individual to demonstrate and learn knowledge and skills" (Dunst, 1991, p. 6).

Often, teacher leadership is viewed as a means to "opt out" of the classroom for formalized administrative positions even though "teachers care less about moving into a few administratively designated leadership positions and more about... enhancing professional aspects of their careers" (Troen & Boles, 1994, p. 282). When teachers opt out of the classroom, school systems lose valuable expertise, and as a result of the frenetic workload that consumes the administrator's workday, it is doubtful that the expertise developed in the classroom will be "put back" into the system once teachers assume administrative positions. However, teachers who emerge as leaders can exert a great deal of influence within their schools, and, given a chance, teacher leaders can "effectively run school units: departments, programs, grade levels, schools within schools, and even whole schools" (Astuto, 1993, p. 25).

Based on research, Sagor and Barnett (1994) provide a portrait of teacher leaders who:

- Are constantly searching for ways to grow personally and professionally.
- Want to maintain the distinction between being a teacher leader and being an administrator.
- Are concerned about maintaining their collegial relationships with other teachers.
- Do not always see themselves as leaders based on their teaching role.
- Believe the school day needs to be restructured and teacher time must be used differently.
- Desire training and professional development to support this new role. (p. 63)

Teacher leaders seek out and actively engage administrators who are in a position to "influence others toward improved educational practices, and identify with and contribute to a community of teacher leaders" (Katzenmeyer & Moller, 1996, p. 6). However, we ask, just what do teacher leaders do?

New Work, New Responsibilities for Teacher Leaders

Extending the discussion on formal and informal leadership, the next logical area to explore appears to be the work and responsibilities of teacher leaders. Regardless of whether teacher leadership is formal or informal, teacher leaders engage in activities that lead to improvement in the schools in which they work—improvement as teachers, improvement in a program or curriculum, and systemic school-wide improvement and change.

Teacher leaders engage in work that requires the development of complex skills, such as group-processing skills, communication skills, and problem-posing and problem-solving skills. Because teacher leaders look beyond their own self-interests, they are often in positions that require them to think beyond the realm of their own classroom and to examine school-wide issues and problems of practice. As department chairs, lead teachers, and grade level leaders, teacher leaders work with and through others to achieve long-term objectives and goals. Teacher leaders not only work with people, but they also work with the curriculum (e.g., leading a workshop on incorporating a new instructional method to complement an aspect of the curriculum). Teacher leaders not only work with personnel in their own buildings, but they also work with personnel from other buildings and with external constituents (e.g., local business leaders).

The reader is asked to reflect about leadership as an opportunity to extend leadership to others. Teachers and others (e.g., principals, assistant principals, department chairs, lead teachers) who are already serving in leadership roles (either formal or informal) have a responsibility to help identify and encourage exemplary teachers to take on new roles as teacher leaders. By cultivating leadership, school systems and their personnel can effectively double, triple, and quadruple the leadership in any given school or system, and this is an empowering thought. Leaders who promote teacher leadership empower teachers by recognizing and acknowledging the competence that this cadre can bring to the learning environment.

Figure 1.2 identifies some of the work of teacher leaders—both the formal and informal roles are inherent, and the skills that are required to accomplish the work parallel what we know about effective leaders—regardless of the position. Teacher leaders assume much of the work they do without leaving the classroom. Supporting their efforts to lead can enhance the possible range of leadership skills and roles.

Figure 1.2. Leadership Roles for Teachers

Teacher Leadership Roles	Range of Skills
Instructional Lead Teacher	Curriculum development, peer coaching, staff development, decision making, risk taking.
Department Chair	Curriculum development, peer coaching, mentoring, staff development, decision making, risk taking.
Committee Chair	Collaboration, shared decision making, risk taking.
Mentor	Peer coaching, reflection, inquiry, problem solving and problem posing, conflict resolution, risk taking.
Teacher/Principal Selection Committee	Decision making, problem solving, conflict resolution, cooperation, risk taking, group processing.
Peer Coach	Mentoring, cooperation, peer coaching, reflection, inquiry, problem solving and problem posing, conflict resolution, risk taking.
Grade Level Leader /or Subject Area Coordinator	Curriculum development, peer coaching, mentoring, staff development, decision making, risk taking, action research (data collection and analysis).
Local School Council Member	Decision making, risk taking.
School Improvement Team Member	Action Research (data collection, analysis), decision making, risk taking.
District-Level Committee Work	Collaboration, shared decision making, risk taking.
After-School Child-Care Coordinator	Collaboration, shared decision making, risk taking.
Club Moderator/Sponsor	Collaboration, shared decision making, risk taking.
Coach	Collaboration, shared decision making, risk taking.
Liaison to the Larger School Community	Communication.

Teacher leaders model inquiry, reflection, and cooperation as they engage in problem solving and decision making. By taking advantage of opportunities to become leaders beyond the confines of the classroom, teacher leaders and supportive administrators will promote growth and development. When leadership is diffused throughout the rank and file of the profession, teachers are in a position to improve not only the capacity for providing even more leadership, but also to improve as classroom teachers—leaders of students.

Leading a school, regardless of its setting, is a complex undertaking. Although principals and assistant principals are in official positions to make decisions, when decision making is diffused among the entire staff, learning occurs for both the people and the organization. That is, both the people and the school as an organization grow together, and the work across the organization is focused more closely on what counts—learning—for the organization and its people: students, teachers, administrators, parents, and those who have a stake in the success of the school—the larger community. The literature on teacher leadership is steeped in empowerment and decision making.

Chapter Summary

The call to teacher leadership inexorably draws teachers toward roles and positions that can have a great effect on the direction of education in schools and districts. Teachers do have the requisite skills to emerge as leaders, and teacher leaders may prove to be one of the most valuable commodities in the schooling enterprise. In fact, for the future of educational leadership, the most exciting and significant growth could occur through the exploration and implementation of models of teacher leadership. There is an authentic and exponential power source available to districts, and teachers are fast becoming ready to assume new responsibilities and challenges. Among the challenges that may arise are some difficult issues that must be identified and dealt with to evolve as a teacher leader.

References

Astuto, T. (Ed.) (1993). *When teachers lead*. New York: Longman.

Dunst, R. (1991, February). *Issues in empowerment*. Paper presented at the annual meeting of Children's Mental Health and Service Policy Convention, Tampa, FL.

Jalongo, M. R. (1991). *Creating learning communities: The role of the teacher in the 21st Century*. Bloomington, IN: National Educational Service.

Katzenmeyer, M., & Moller, G. (1996). *Awakening the sleeping giant: Leadership development for teachers*. Newbury Park, CA: Corwin Press.

Lambert, L. (1998). *Building leadership capacity in schools*. Alexandria, VA: Association for Supervision and Curriculum Development.

Lieberman, A., & Miller, L. (1999). *Teachers—transforming their world and their work*. New York: Teachers College Press.

Lightfoot, S. L. (1986). On goodness in schools: Themes of empowerment. *Peabody Journal of Education, 63*(3), 9–28.

Méndez-Morse, S. (1992). *Leadership characteristics that facilitate change*. Austin, TX: Southwest Educational Development Laboratory.

Romanish, B. (1991). Teacher empowerment: The litmus test of school restructuring. *Social Science Record, 28*(1), 55–69.

Sagor, R., & Barnett, B. G. (1994). *The TQE principal: A transformed leader.* Thousand Oaks, CA: Corwin Press.

Troen, V., & Boles, K. (1994). Two teachers examine the power of teacher leadership. In D. R. Walling (Ed.), *Teachers as leaders: Perspectives on the professional development of teachers* (pp. 275–286). Bloomington, IN: Phi Delta Kappa Educational Foundation.

UCLA School Management Program Academies. (n.d.). Developing teacher leadership. Los Angeles, CA. Retrieved July 3, 2002, from http://www.smp.gseis.ucla.edu/smp/programs/ILA/leadership.html

2

The Thorny Issues of Teacher Leadership

In this Chapter

- Lines of authority: Are teacher leaders powerless leaders?
- Isolation
- Role conflict and role ambiguity
- Resolving conflicts
- Teacher leaders and higher-level decision making: Inclusion or intrusion?

Introducing Difficulties of Being a Teacher Leader

Teacher leaders are in a unique position to learn more about their craft, to share knowledge with their colleagues, and to become conduits for sparking change at the site level. Perhaps more profoundly, teacher leaders create opportunities for more teachers to be leaders. For teacher leaders, leadership means entry into the world of high-level decision making. Although all teachers are leaders, there is a difference between formal and informal teacher leadership. The more formal the leadership position (e.g., lead teacher, department chair), the more formal authority the teacher leader assumes. As teacher leaders are included in levels of school-site operations, the probability of conflict also increases.

Being a teacher leader means understanding the role of teacher leader and being willing and able to navigate the unpredictable waters of conflict, power, and politics. The purposes of this chapter are to identify some of the potential difficulties associated with being a teacher leader and to offer some possible strategies for handling those difficulties.

Lines of Authority: Are Teacher Leaders Powerless Leaders?

Teacher leaders are given responsibility for a set of tasks usually prescribed in an officially approved job description. These tasks can include purchasing and distributing supplies, representing teachers or programs before outside stakeholders, and providing instructional leadership through such activities as supervising instruction, coaching novice teachers, coordinating textbook adoptions, and aligning curriculum to state-wide learning objectives. Often included in a teacher leader's job description is such information as to whom the teacher leader reports, the qualifications needed to hold the position, and a broad description of expectations and benefits, such as release time or a stipend. However, these job descriptions rarely clarify for teacher leaders just how much power they do and do not have. The concept of power is complex and can be clarified by examining the types of power and then by discussing how power can influence, negatively or positively, the work of teacher leaders as they interact with others at the site and beyond.

In the literature, the seven most common types of power include: (a) reward power, (b) coercive power, (c) legitimate power, (d) expert power, (e) referent power, (f) informational power, and (g) connection power. Each one of these types of power are characterized by what one has or does to exert power with, through, or over a person, situation, or event.

French and Raven (1959) identified five different types of power:

1. *Reward power* is based on the ability a person has to give rewards. "The strength of reward power increases with the magnitude of the rewards" (p. 156). Essentially, the more rewards a person has to give, the more power the person has *over* others.

2. *Coercive power* is similar to reward power in that it also involves the "ability to manipulate ... [punishment] if [the object of the manipulation] fails to conform ..." (p. 157). Coercive power is power *over* people in which a person can "force" other people to do something against their will.

3. *Legitimate power* stems from internalized values that "dictate that [a person] has a legitimate right to influence another [person]." (p. 159)

4. *Expert power* is based on "knowledge or perception that [one person] attributes to [another] within a given area" (p. 163). If a person has well-developed skills or expertise in a particular area, that person derives power from the knowledge or skill in which he excels.

5. *Referent power* is based on attraction or prestige. "In some cases, attraction or prestige may have a specific basis, and the range of the referent power will be limited accordingly" (p. 163).

Later, Raven and Kruglanski (1970) identified an additional source of power:

6. *Informational power* results from "providing information not previously available to another person or by pointing out contingencies of which the other person had not been aware" (p. 73).

The seventh source of power, connection power, identified by Hersey (1984), is worth examining in light of the work that teacher leaders do.

7. *Connection power* is "based on the followers' perceiving the leader to be connected to an influential or important person inside or outside of the organization" (p. 79).

The following discussion offers a look at each type of power and its impact on the role and the work of teacher leaders. Power can be positive or negative and much of the value placed on power resides in the specific context in which power is used. As a caveat, we share with you what is written on a sign hanging on a principal's wall: "POWER—Once You Use It, You Lose It."

Reward Power

For the teacher leader, reward power is usually limited. This limitation depends on how much discretion the teacher leader is given over the resources available from the school. Reward power can be an effective tool in furthering teacher and student learning; however, teacher leaders need to be careful in deciding when and how to use reward power. By funding a colleague's program out of the departmental or grade level budget, teacher leaders exercise reward power. This use of reward power could have a divisive effect on the department or grade level that results from jealousy or a perception of favoritism. The teacher who receives the funding tends to view the teacher leader through a more favorable light whereas other department or grade level members could view the teacher leader as playing favorites. The teacher leader can help prevent divisiveness by establishing a policy for the dispersion of funds.

Perhaps most importantly, teacher leaders can use reward power to support their colleagues. For example, teacher leaders can use their release time to teach a colleague's class, thus creating extra release time for teachers to engage in professional activities. This extra time could be used to attend a professional conference, to observe another teacher, or to meet with a peer coach. By rotating release time among all members of the team or department, teacher leaders provide equity of resources.

Coercive Power

Coercive power is, by definition, the power to punish. Administrators must sometimes resort to coercive power: dealing with an unruly child, working with an uncooperative teacher, or correcting an unreliable support staff member. Through budgetary discretion, teacher leaders could use coercive power; however, coercive power should be used with great caution. Coercive power is rooted in a clearly delineated hierarchy in which one member of the organization is vested with the responsibility for another's performance. Because principals are accountable for the quality of instruction in classrooms, they have the authority to employ punishment, if necessary, to correct teaching deficiencies. It would be unusual for a teacher leader's job description to provide this type of authority. Those who use coercive power manipulate people and the system to "win" their way. Coercive power strips others of any real authority to make decisions.

Legitimate Power

Legitimate power is dependent on the acceptance of a person's authority, and this type of power is solely based on that person's position within the organization. Administrators have legitimate power and use it daily. For the teacher leader, legitimate power is based on the sometimes-slippery language of job descriptions and faculty handbooks. Unfortunately, teacher leaders have little or no input into the writing of job descriptions or faculty handbooks.

Further, in many situations, the extent of a teacher leader's legitimate power is determined by the culture and climate of the school. What are the administrative team's expectations of teacher leaders? How well do the administrators support the work of teacher leaders? Do the "rank and file" teachers accept these expectations? The answers to these questions can assist teacher leaders to define the extent of their legitimate power. As with other types of power, teacher leaders need to be seen by their colleagues as using their power to support teacher learning and to build trust.

Expert Power

Because teacher leaders enjoy the advantage of either content expertise and proximity (department chairs) or grade level proximity and expertise (team leader or grade level leader), they are viewed as experts. As such, one tool at their disposal for "getting things done" is expert power. For example, the chair of the mathematics department *is also a mathematics teacher*; therefore, this teacher leader has experience and knowledge of the curriculum, content, and methods involved in teaching mathematics. Because many teacher leaders teach in a district before assuming a formal leadership role, they are also familiar with the culture and expectations of teachers.

Expert power can be a valuable tool for the teacher leader. Through mentoring and inducting new teachers, the teacher leader's expertise and experience become a "living reference book of teaching" for the novice. By training other department, team, or grade level members to be mentors, teacher leaders extend themselves by empowering colleagues to also be teacher leaders. By sharing expert power with their colleagues (acknowledging their expertise), teacher leaders are less likely to fall into the trap called arrogance. All teachers have expertise, and teacher leaders are able to "tap" into the strengths of their teaching colleagues.

Referent Power

Others view leaders, who have referent power, as having a special attractiveness or prestige that can influence others to action. Simply through the "power of the personality," these leaders are able to motivate others in the organization to work toward common goals. Because referent power is dependent primarily on personal traits, neither job descriptions nor administrative expectations can lend significant support for it. Referent power emanates from strong "people" skills.

For the teacher leader, referent power can be a powerful tool. By modeling professional, supportive behaviors that empower others to be leaders, teacher leaders can exert a strong influence among their grade level, team, or department members. When teacher leaders share power, they can become stronger leaders because of their status in the organization, and their push to empower others.

Informational Power

Sir Frances Bacon wrote in *Meditationes Sacrae* (Sacred Meditation, 1597) "knowledge is power." The source of informational power is, of course, information. Think of the types of information a teacher leader has and what disclosure of certain information could mean. Figure 2.1 highlights the types of information that teacher leaders often have.

Figure 2.1. Sources of Case-Sensitive Information for Teacher Leaders

Student:	Test scores, discipline records, counseling files, records from classroom observations.
Teacher:	Prior teaching evaluation ratings and reports, classroom observation reports, profile of student performance on standardized tests, certain personnel records, information shared at administrative and/or team or department meetings, lesson plans, record books.
Administrative:	Meeting summaries, comments made at meetings, memos.

As with other types of power, informational power can also cause great harm if used improperly. The type and quality of the information being used, as well as the motivation for sharing, are important determiners of any use of informational power. Information should be shared to support student and teacher learning. Informational power should never be used as a conduit for gossip, to broker favors, or to leverage dependency.

Informational power is exercised when important information is shared with those who do not already have the information, but have a need to know. When teachers are "included" through the sharing of information, especially in decision-making processes, they become empowered professionals. As empowered professionals, teachers are able to make data-driven decisions about student learning and their own professional learning, in addition to making valuable contributions in areas that have been traditionally reserved for administrators (e.g., interviewing teaching candidates).

Connection Power

Few people discount the importance of networking. Unfortunately, few institutions are less amenable to connecting people than schools. Just as the walls of classrooms divide one classroom from the next, the structure of schools and the work teachers do divide *one teacher from the next*. Moreover, the demands on teachers tend to isolate them from nearly every major group of stakeholders—parents, community leaders, and even the administrators in their own buildings. Teacher leaders, when properly supported, are ideally situated to help connect teachers to each other.

Although "being connected" throughout the school is important, connections can be misused. Teacher leaders need to be cognizant of the power that can come from perceived connections—for example, the connection between teacher leaders and administrators. As with other power bases, teacher leaders need to take great care in disseminating information and resources received from administrators. All teachers need to be kept connected through the flow of information and resources; however, no teacher leader should provide favorable treatment to any teacher based on a "special" connection they may share.

The "Magic" of Power

Power shared is power multiplied; power hoarded is powerless. The real magic of power lies in its ability to multiply as more people within a school have access to it. When administrators empower teacher leaders to lead, and teacher leaders share their power and empower their colleagues, a remarkable transformation can occur. Instead of a collection of isolated workers disconnected from one another, the school can become a learning community with people connected by a common purpose and vision for learning.

Isolation

Teachers are often isolated from each other, from administrators, from counselors, and from stakeholders outside the school building. Teachers have too readily accepted isolation as "the norm" in schools. As a result, according to Lortie (1975):

> Teachers attach great meaning to the boundaries which separate their classrooms from the rest of the school and, of course, the community. Teachers deprecate transactions which cut across those boundaries. Walls are perceived as beneficial; they protect and enhance the course of instruction. All but teacher and students are outsiders...other adults have potential for hindrance but not for help. (p. 169)

Teachers are caught in the tension between the desire to be autonomous and the need to learn from each other. Fullan (1993) asserts that:

> The professional isolation of teachers limits access to new ideas and better solutions, drives stress inward to fester and accumulate, fails to recognize and praise success, and permits incompetence to exist and persist to the detriment of students, colleagues, and the teachers themselves. Isolation allows...conservatism and resistance to innovation in teaching. (p. 34)

Finding a solution to this tension can be problematic. Teachers need to share expertise and problems with one another; yet, they need to retain their sense of individual identity. The stress that comes from isolation can also lead to burnout. Teacher leaders can play a crucial role in assisting a grade level, team, or department to find the fertile ground of collaboration that exists between the unproductive extremes of isolation and autonomy.

Teacher Leaders as Trust-Builders

If collaborative learning is to replace the isolation that exists in many schools, teacher leaders need to become trust-builders. Learning together involves risk. Teachers have to "let down their guards" and allow each other to see the "warts" of their teaching practices. At the same time, teachers need to be able to recognize and to accept each other's strengths without being threatened by them. For this type of risk taking to be successful, teachers must trust each other. Strategies for building trust between colleagues include: maintaining open communication, finding time for team building, and inducting new team, grade level, or department members to the school, its culture and norms.

Maintaining Open Communication

Communication in schools occurs through a complex collection of communication networks. These networks include communication within groups of stakeholders such as administrators, teacher leaders, and teachers, as well as communication between each of these groups. Additionally, communication in schools travels through both formal (e.g., memos, newsletters, e-mail listserves, radio/television stations, and web sites) and informal channels (e.g., talk in the hallways, faculty lounge, and other places where teachers meet). Effective teacher leaders are aware of the many communication networks in their schools and know how and when to use them.

Perhaps the most important way teacher leaders can build trust in grade levels, teams, and departments is to know when administrative intervention is and is not needed. If every word spoken between a teacher and a teacher leader finds its way to an administrator, teacher leaders develop the reputation of being a "spy" or a "snitch," and then teacher leaders lose credibility with their colleagues. In the same vein, a teacher leader needs discretion about sharing communications with other teachers. Without trust, grade levels, teams, and departments lose their effectiveness to support learning and what each member of the community does to enhance this learning.

High school department chairs, elementary school instructional coordinators, and middle school lead teachers often serve as a liaison between the administration and other teachers. Often, this role puts teacher leaders in the middle. On the one hand, they need to be supportive of the administration, and on the other hand, they need to be supportive of teachers. This position in the middle can make teacher leaders privy to a great deal of information. Maintaining confidences, while simultaneously keeping the communication lines open, potentially puts teacher leaders in the position of navigating the tightrope between open communication and irresponsible leaking of information.

Finding Time for Team Building

In many schools, the boundaries of time are as isolating as the walls between classrooms. Teachers spend the majority of their days either delivering instruction or planning for it. In addition to instructional matters, teachers attend to duty periods, club meetings, and periodic faculty meetings. In too many schools, too little time remains in the day for teachers' learning. If time is to be set aside for teachers, purposeful effort must be made to find that time—it does not simply appear. To find sufficient learning time for teachers, teacher leaders need to look both within and outside the school day for the solution.

Judicious use of substitute teachers, paraprofessionals, and teacher aides can help create additional learning time during the school day for teacher learning. Teacher leaders who are afforded extra release time can use that time to free other teachers for important learning. Additionally, time set aside during the school day for grade level or team meetings must be used wisely—for learning—not as verbal memos. Dissemination of information via memos and e-mail helps to conserve meeting time for discussion between teachers and for team building.

In addition to time together during the school day, valuable team building can occur outside the school day. Although teachers are usually not legally obligated to participate in functions held outside school hours, effective teacher leaders should not close their eyes to the opportunities for growth in after-hours events. Two types of events can be of particular benefit: social events and working events. Social events, held away from the school, can assist teachers to get to know one another better in a nonthreatening environment. The better teachers get to know one another, the more comfortable they will become with one another, and the more they will begin to trust each other. Although building relationships with teachers and administrators is very important, the teacher leader needs to be careful not to become blinded by social relationships, and the possibility of teachers or administrators trying to use social relationships to curry favors.

In addition to social events, more structured get-togethers outside of school hours can help teachers "gel" as a grade level, team, or department. These events could be held at a conference center or a meeting room at a restaurant. A retreat held a few days before the beginning of school can help the grade level, team, or department get off on the "right foot." Figure 2.2 offers a sample agenda for this type of event.

Figure 2.2. Science Department Pre-School Retreat

Agenda

August 10, 2002

- Meal (or gathering with refreshments)
- Ice Breaker (to introduce teachers to one another)
- Staff Development (learning plans for the year)
- Curricular Issues/Teaching Assignments
- Site Goals and Integration of Departmental Goals
- Classroom Management Plans
- Open Discussion

By assisting teachers to get to know and trust each other outside of the school environment, trust can be built during the hectic day-to-day work environment where little time can be found to talk and interact with each other.

Inducting New Members

Experienced teachers new to a school need help with learning the school's routines and culture. Teachers new to the profession will need even more assistance. New surroundings can make even the most seasoned of veterans feel alone and isolated. For first year teachers, *everything is* new, and the stress is amplified. A well-structured induction plan can help alleviate the stress and isolation experienced by new members of the team. The role of the teacher leader in inducting new teachers needs to include:

- Ensuring the new teacher has a copy of the site faculty handbook. New teachers need to learn many procedures: recording attendance, referring students for discipline, handling money, distributing textbooks, and getting equipment repaired or replaced.

- Giving the new teacher a tour of the campus. New teachers will need to be able to find the mailboxes, copy machine, administrative offices, counseling offices, lunchroom, duty stations, and much more.

- Assigning the new teacher a mentor. Induction is a process, not an isolated event. New teachers, whether new to the building or new to the profession, need to know that someone is concerned about them.

Having a colleague on whom they can depend can help smooth the otherwise bumpy road experienced by new teachers.

Isolation and Burnout

Stress from isolation from colleagues, when combined with the inherent tension between teaching and administrative tasks, can lead to burnout. Although there will be times when the teacher leader will burn the candle at both ends, the teacher leader will need to give to other pursuits as well. Time spent with family or outside interests or hobbies can actually serve as a rejuvenator. Maintaining a balance between all of the activities will assist the teacher leader to be more effective with unlimited longevity.

There are some specific strategies that can aid in avoiding burnout and that can promote leadership that is more effective. Planning and preparing for leadership is essential to conserving future time and energy. Sharing certain leadership duties with other teachers can relieve some of the most time-consuming elements of a project. In addition, routing some of the tasks associated with a project to office personnel can serve to widen participation as well as alleviate some of the "nonessential," but important work that must be done. The teacher leader might also consider the use of parents and even well trained students to take over appropriate jobs that will enable the teacher leader to focus on more pressing areas of concern. In the case of sharing tasks and duties with others, the use of time management strategies may actually turn out to be a very effective form of leadership in itself.

Teacher Leaders and the Nature of Isolation

The very nature of schools promotes the isolation of teachers. Teacher leaders can take the lead in breaking down the walls of isolation in schools. Using substitute teachers, paraprofessionals, and their own release time, teacher leaders can help find needed learning time within the school day for their colleagues. Well-planned, judiciously scheduled out-of-school retreats and social events can help support the teacher leader's in-school efforts at trust building. The thorny nature of isolation lies in the difficulty of navigating the fine line between encouraging collaboration and being seen as an intruder by teachers who are protective of their "turf"—their classrooms. Teacher leaders need to celebrate the individual expertise and experience of each teacher, while encouraging teachers to contribute that expertise and experience to the common good. This thorny issue is further complicated by the "dual nature" and characteristic of the world of teacher leaders—the need for teacher leaders to be both teachers and quasi-administrators.

Role Conflict and Role Ambiguity

Although teacher leaders are, and should be, leaders, they are still, first and foremost, *teachers*. High school department chairs, middle-level team leaders, elementary school grade level leaders, and other teacher leaders facilitate curriculum development, coordinate textbook adoption efforts, and plan and conduct staff development, all in addition to planning and delivering instruction for their own classes. Many times, teacher leaders are provided little or no "extra" release time to complete these noninstructional tasks. This "dual identity" as both teacher and administrator can create high levels of stress for teacher leaders because, in too many situations, they are not fully accepted by either the teaching faculty or the administrative team. Vaguely written job descriptions and poorly written site and district policies serve only to exacerbate the role conflict and role ambiguity seemingly inherent in formal teacher leadership positions.

A role, according to Huse (1980) is "the sum total of expectations placed on individuals by supervisors, peers, subordinates, vendors, customers, and others, depending on the particular job" (p. 53). Katz and Kahn (1978) define role conflict as "the simultaneous occurrence of two or more role expectations such that compliance with one would make compliance with the other more difficult" (p. 204). For teacher leaders, the expectations of teaching (planning lessons, designing assessments, managing the classroom) must coexist with the expectations of being a leader outside the classroom. These roles present conflict for the teacher leader on three fronts: (a) time, (b) relationships with colleagues, and (c) competing demands from the site and the district.

Time

The amount of release time afforded to teacher leaders varies somewhat from district to district. Because of dwindling resources, less release time seems to be the trend. The lack of release time forces teacher leaders to make difficult choices in prioritizing tasks that need to be done.

Most teacher leaders tend to give their teaching responsibilities top priority, thus limiting the time available for leadership outside of the classroom. Although the teacher leader's students are better for being the number one priority, teacher leaders can still find themselves in a "Catch-22" situation. Regardless of the amount of time teacher leaders are required to teach, they must still find time to accomplish such tasks as managing inventories, developing site and district curriculum materials, and assisting other teachers. Many times, wherever possible, teacher leaders end up taking work home. This can create added stress for teacher leaders and their families.

Relationships with Colleagues

In some cases, accepting a leadership role outside of the classroom does result in teacher leaders receiving benefits not generally afforded to their colleagues. Among these benefits are release time, extra funding for professional conferences, and more input into selection of teaching assignments. These benefits, though important for supporting the teacher leader's work, can cause a rift between teacher leaders and their colleagues. How a teacher leader handles such situations can have a major impact on how effective a leader she or he can be.

Perhaps the best strategy for handling relationships between teacher leaders and other teachers is for the teacher leader to never exploit any benefits received solely by virtue of being a teacher leader. For example, being a teacher leader does not necessarily have to affect the teaching assignments within a department, team, or grade level. The addition of only "good classes" to the teacher leader's schedule can signal unequal treatment in teaching assignments. Neither should the teacher leader attempt to take on all of the most difficult teaching assignments. Such action could interfere with the teacher leader's out-of-the-classroom responsibilities, and professional well-being.

Managing Competing Site/District Demands

Many times, teacher leaders serve on site or district committees. Membership on site and district committees creates an additional time drain for the teacher leader: attending meetings, collecting data, writing reports, preparing applications for grants, and making presentations. For the teacher leader, membership on these committees can be an obligation; it can also introduce new levels of conflict.

Teacher leaders are, in most cases, full-time teachers and part-time administrators. When committee work is added to the teacher leader's already hectic schedule, "something has to give" if this tension is to be resolved. Because teacher leaders normally view themselves as teachers first, administrative work and committee work sometimes may not receive the teacher leader's best efforts. As a result, the teacher leader's working relationship with the site or district administrator responsible for the committee's work can become strained.

In addition to the time squeeze it presents, committee work can create conflicts of purpose. This thorny issue can be especially difficult if the committee is a district-level committee. If the central administrator overseeing the committee's work has a strained relationship with the teacher leader's site administrator, or if the committee's purpose runs counter to an initiative favored by the teacher leader's principal, the teacher leader can find herself trying to stay balanced on an unsteady, political tightrope.

Resolving Conflicts

In any workplace, conflict is always possible. With rising levels of accountability and ever tightening resources, schools can be become "hotbeds" of conflict. Conflict can result from many underlying causes. Schmuck and Runkel (1994) identified five sources of conflict among educators:

1. Differentiation of function among parts of the educational organization;
2. Power struggles between persons and subsystems;
3. Role conflicts;
4. Differences in interpersonal style among educators; and
5. Stress imposed on the educational organization by external forces. (p. 331)

Teacher leaders can assist in the resolution of each of these types of conflict.

Differentiation of Function among Parts of the Educational Organization

Today's schools are complex organizations with counseling departments, food service crews, and, in many school districts, police departments and medical clinics. All of these groups interact with teachers and administrators. Despite these interactions, it is unlikely that any group will be aware of all of the circumstances of another's work. This natural information gap exists in many organizations and can be a source of conflict.

For example, a high school principal spends an inordinate amount of time outside of the building soliciting the support of local businesses for her school. The mathematics teachers believe that the principal is neglecting the students and teachers through her absence from the building, especially considering the relative lack of experience of the three assistant principals. How can the department chair help resolve the growing rift between the math teachers and the principal?

Several strategies are available to the math department chair. The math department chair could call a meeting to explain the need to search for additional sources for funding of school projects. In addition to the department meeting, the department chair might consider having either the principal or one of the assistant principals speak with the math teachers to reassure them of administrative support. The department chair should also maintain a higher presence during his release time. By clearly communicating details of the situation, reassuring the department members of continuing support, and maintaining visibility, the conflict can be resolved through the proactive work the department chair does.

Power Struggles between Persons and Subsystems

A second source of conflict in schools comes from power struggles between persons or groups within the school. This type of conflict often results from a struggle over a limited resource such as building space, teachers' time, or funding. To illustrate, consider a middle school with six teams: two sixth grade teams, two seventh grade teams, and two eighth grade teams. The school has only one vocal music teacher. Because the vocal music teacher is itinerant and travels to another school in the district, she is only available to teach classes during the morning hours. Both the sixth grade teams and the eighth grade teams want their students to have vocal music during the early morning slot. What can the team leaders do to resolve the conflict?

A resolution of this conflict could begin with the sixth and eighth grade team leaders meeting and discussing the reasons why each team believes its students need to have vocal music during the first hour. The team leaders also need to decide whether the vocal music teacher needs to be involved in the discussion. A possible resolution to this conflict would be a compromise in which the sixth and eighth grades alternate having vocal music during the first period. Regardless of the solution, without the teacher leaders taking action, this conflict between the sixth grade teachers and the eighth grade teachers could result in a rift between the groups, causing difficult-to-repair damage to the faculty as a whole.

Role Conflicts

The existence of roles and the conflicts that multiple roles can create for teacher leaders has been discussed earlier in this chapter. However, what happens when a teacher's interpretation of the expectations of his role are in conflict with that of the person responsible for supervising him? Consider the following situation in which role conflict plays havoc between a teacher and a teacher leader. The second grade teachers met to plan the implementation of a new strategy for teaching reading. One teacher decided that he could vary the approach by using a group-oriented approach, as opposed to an individual approach, and still be able to work within the expectations of his colleagues. How might the grade level leader solve this conflict? On the one hand, the second grade teacher is meeting the objective—he is teaching the skills and the content of the curriculum, but on the other hand, he is dismissing the approach that the second grade team decided on—individual instruction.

The grade level leader first needs to decide if her colleague's variation is consistent with the expectations she and the administrators have for the new reading program. There are some strategies available to the grade level leader if she believes there is a conflict that must be resolved. First, the grade level leader can meet one-on-one with the teacher to discuss the variation in teaching strategy to determine if it is workable. An alternate strategy would be for the grade level leader to have a grade level meeting to discuss the possibility of using the alternate technique. The grade level leader will need to consider the culture of the school and the relationships between the second grade teachers in deciding which strategy to use. Regardless of which approach is chosen, the grade level leader is in a position to try to resolve the conflict, and, at the same time, help to strengthen the second grade teachers as a group. However, what happens if the grade level leader cannot resolve the issue, and the second grade teachers begin to splinter in their approaches to teaching reading? What options does the grade level leader have available besides running to an administrator?

Essentially, the grade level leader needs to keep the "talk" among teachers moving forward, provide resources that examine the relative worth and value of each approach, and to track and share results of both approaches. At some point, the grade level leader may need to involve the administration, but this should be a last resort. The grade level leader, the middle school team leader, the high school department chair, or any other teacher in a leadership position will lose credibility among other teachers if he or she continually "runs" to the administration.

Differences in Interpersonal Style among Educators

Schools are comprised of individuals that bring to the group individual needs, experiences, and methods of getting things done. Sometimes, these differences can create conflict. For example, veteran teachers bring different learning needs, teaching experiences, and a wider range of instructional techniques to the group than those brought to the school setting by novice teachers. Consider the following situation.

The high school English Department set a departmental goal of incorporating more cooperative learning activities and implementing authentic assessment to assess writing skills. One department member felt very uncomfortable with the idea of trying to learn to use new instructional techniques and to design new assessments. However, these goals were consistent with site and district goals. This conflict was exacerbated by pressure from the principal on the department chair to get the "holdout" to agree to work toward these goals. What strategies could the English Department chair use to find a resolution to this conflict?

Because learning these skills is essential to achieving site and district goals, the English Department chair must convince the "holdout" teacher to embrace the goals of learning to incorporate cooperative learning and to design authentic student assessments. Perhaps the most effective strategy for the teacher leader in this situation would be to have a private meeting with the "holdout" teacher. In a private meeting, the department chair is more likely to discover the real issue making this teacher uncomfortable. By resolving the hidden issue, the "holdout" can be encouraged to join the team. However, if this teacher will not reveal why he is uncomfortable or unwilling to comply, then perhaps administrative intervention is necessary. However, resorting to administrative intervention too early in the process could alienate the teacher. If possible, the department chair needs to keep the lines of communication open and try to solve the issue without running to the principal as the "first-line" defense.

Stress Imposed on the Educational Organization by External Forces

Recently, federal legislation raised the bar of accountability for schools. Other recent trends have begun tying accountability measures to funding and, in some areas, to teacher evaluation. Each new statute seems to raise the level of stress among teachers and administrators. Elevated stress levels and finding the best way to alleviate that stress can lead to conflict. The following scenario illustrates this type of conflict.

The state legislature has passed a new law that requires all students to be reading on grade level by the time they complete the third grade. The new law has the full endorsement of the state board of education. The site's grade level leaders schedule a meeting to discuss strategies consistent with the new mandate. Some grade level leaders express doubt as to the school's ability to meet the mandate. Among the problems that immediately surface are the low socioeconomic level of the majority of students, an unusually large number of identified special education students in this year's first grade, and the lack of financial resources to pay for new teaching materials. What can the grade level leaders do to assist in solving this problem?

The resolution of this conflict must begin with the grade level leaders who are confident in the school's ability to meet the new mandate. Because the district has no alternative but to meet the new mandate, all grade level leaders must join the effort to comply. The thorny issue for the grade level leaders already "on board" is to find a way to support the doubters and, at the same time, value their opinion, and then win them over to join in the work needed to accomplish the goal of getting students to read at grade level. In the end, the grade level leaders have to work together as a unit; they need to send a unified message that they are working toward the same end, regardless of differences in opinion.

Teacher Leaders and Higher-Level Decision Making: Inclusion or Intrusion?

Although tasks such as inventorying textbooks, conducting meetings, and building teams are important, many teachers seek to transcend the more common tasks of teacher leaders. They desire involvement and recognition in the higher levels of decision making at the site and district levels. This is, perhaps, the greatest challenge for teacher leaders.

Teacher Leaders and Higher-Level Decision Making

Higher-level decision making is, perhaps, the area of school operations that presents the most number of potential "thorns" for the teacher leader. The reasons for this seem clear. First, of all levels of decision making at the site level, the stakes involved in personnel and budget decisions are the highest. Second, because the stakes are so high, personnel and budgetary decisions represent the highest levels of control at the school site. Third, many administrators view these decisions as their exclusive territory.

Like teachers, administrators bring a wide range of experiences to their work. Most building principals are former teachers, have taken graduate coursework in administration, and have served as assistant principals. All of these experiences shape the way an administrator approaches the work of the principalship. These attitudes normally have a profound effect on the role of teacher leaders especially in making high-stakes decisions such as those in the areas of personnel and the budget. The principal can make the difference between the "inclusion" of or the "intrusion" of teacher leaders in high-stakes decision making.

The Inclusion of Teacher Leaders in Higher-Level Decision Making

Principals who subscribe to shared governance share power with teachers and invite them to participate in making personnel and budgetary decisions for the school. Although final authority for these decisions still rests with the principal, in most cases, the input of teacher leaders is given significant weight in those decisions. With the opportunity for teacher leaders to participate in personnel and budgetary decisions comes a heightened level of responsibility. This added level of responsibility introduces more thorny issues for the teacher leader: accepting administrative "override" of group decisions and maintaining the confidentiality of highly sensitive information needed to make better decisions.

In schools where governance is shared, most hiring decisions begin with an interview of a teacher candidate conducted by a group that includes both administrators and teacher leaders. Budgetary decisions also include input from teacher leaders. Despite the participation of others in the decision-making process, the final decision still rests with the principal. Although most principals support the recommendation of interviewing committees, there can be occasions where the principal may have to "override" the group decision based on information to which only she is privy. Teacher leaders need to be able to accept decision overrides as a legitimate exercise of administrative responsibility and not as an attack on the group's ability to make decisions.

For the teacher leader, the first opportunity to participate in interviewing teacher candidates or in budget discussions with administrators can result in a mixture of emotions. The teacher leader normally experiences exhilaration and a sense of increased importance and, at the same time, some apprehension because the process is so new. In such matters, confidentiality is essential. Therefore, teacher leaders need to resist the urge to share "all that is going on" with everyone else in the school. The release of confidential information can result in teacher colleagues expressing hard or hurt feelings toward the teacher leader. A teacher leader may even be blamed for a department member's friend not being recommended for a teaching position, or for a grade level initiative not being funded. In addition, the trust needed within the decision-making group could be compromised if information is shared out of context. Teacher leaders need to allow principals to orchestrate the release of information.

Intrusion into Higher-Level Decision Making: Working with Principals

Many teacher leaders want an active role in the higher-level decision-making process of their school, and some principals welcome the insights and perspectives that teacher leaders can bring to the mix. However, some principals perceive teachers who have these aspirations as intrusions (at best), or worse, as threats. Before a teacher leader attempts to gain entry into higher-level decision making, it is critical for the teacher leader to determine whether the principal views the teacher leader as a welcome professional, an intruder, or as a threat. If the principal perceives teacher leaders to be merely intrusions, there can be some limited opportunities for involvement in higher-level decision making. If, on the other hand, the teacher leader is believed to be a threat, little or no opportunity for real involvement is likely.

Two possible strategies for teacher leaders who want to "intrude" into higher-level decision making exist. We refer to the first as "informal" leadership and to the second as "underground" leadership. Informal leadership occurs when the teacher leader makes informal recommendations, either in writing or verbally, to the administrator. Because these recommendations are normally unsolicited, there is usually little opportunity for the teacher leader to do any meaningful follow-up. Because the teacher leader is using the "chain of command," the risk of retribution is normally limited.

Practicing "underground" leadership requires the teacher leader to find alternatives to the normal chain of command. Using this strategy, teacher leaders make recommendations through other people, such as a site faculty member or an off-site administrator that the teacher leader trusts *and* that "has the ear" of the principal. Obviously, trust is paramount in this scenario and the potential risks are high. A high level of discretion is necessary when attempting to work with the autocratic principal. The teacher leader must keep in mind that the principal establishes the ground rules for the school. However, teachers who are leaders have the courage of their convictions and skills to properly express them.

There are numerous ways in which teacher leaders experience tension between their work as a teacher and their work in the position they hold in the school. Case-sensitive information must not be used as a way of holding something over another teacher or as a way to coerce teachers into complying with the wishes of others. Teacher leaders will struggle with the work that they do, but perhaps the struggle is worth it if teacher leadership is to be "iterative" (Lieberman & Miller, 1999, p. 22), with teacher leaders empowering other teachers to become leaders. This is the real work of the teacher leadership.

Chapter Summary

Teacher leaders can be a critical link between teachers and administrators. However, to be that link, teacher leaders must learn to navigate the often-murky waters of school politics, conflict, role ambiguity, and isolation. The navigational tools most important to the teacher leader's work are clear communication and trust building. Through clear communication, teacher leaders can keep all teachers informed about how they can help to further site and district goals, as well as to assist in finding staff development opportunities to support teachers' efforts to improve in the classroom.

Open communication also helps to build trust. Information can be used to either include people or exclude people from a team. By keeping everyone "on the inside," no teacher should feel like an outsider. When everyone is an insider, trust develops. When trust is the norm, isolation dissipates. Teacher leaders who want to go beyond the norm know that the road to participation in higher-level decision making goes through the principal's office. The secret to successful navigation of this road depends on the attitudes of the principal and the ability of teacher leaders to identify and avoid the potholes—the thorny issues of teacher leadership.

References

French, J. R., & Raven, B. H. (1959). The bases of social power. In D. Cartwright (Ed.), *Studies in social power* (pp. 150–167). Ann Arbor, MI: The University of Michigan Press.

Fullan, M. G. (1993). *Change forces: Probing the depths of educational reform.* London, UK: Falmer Press.

Hersey, P. (1984). *The situational leader.* Escondito, CA: The Center for Leadership Studies.

Huse, E. F. (1980). *Organizational development and change.* (2nd ed.). St. Paul, MN: West.

Katz, D., & Kahn, R. L. (1978). *The social psychology of organizations.* (2nd ed.). New York: John Wiley and Sons.

Lieberman, A., & Miller, L. (1999). *Teachers—transforming their world and their work.* New York: Teachers College Press.

Lortie, D. C. (1975). *Schoolteacher: A sociological study.* Chicago: The University of Chicago Press.

Raven, B. H., & Kruglanski, A. W. (1970). Conflict and power. In P. Swingle (Ed.), *The structure of conflict* (pp. 69–105). New York: Academic Press.

Schmuck, R. A., & Runkel, P. J. (1994). *The handbook of organizational development in schools and colleges.* (4th ed.). Prospect Heights, IL: Waveland Press.

3

Teacher Leadership in the Elementary School

In this Chapter

- ♦ Partnerships with Parents
- ♦ Vertical Teaming: Laying the Curricular Foundation
- ♦ The Work of Grade Level Leaders
- ♦ Coordinating the Work of Teachers Across Grade Levels
- ♦ The Work of a Teacher Facilitator
- ♦ The Unique Relationship between a Teacher Facilitator and the Principal

Introducing Teacher Leadership at the Elementary Level

The basic premise of this book is that all teachers are leaders and that leadership is not for only those who have an official title. Teacher leadership occurs many times throughout the day by a variety of teachers. At the elementary level, there are formal teacher leadership positions—lead teacher, teacher facilitator, grade level leader—and probably yet-to-be crafted titles. And there are informal leadership roles for teachers who share their expertise with others when they present at a conference, mentor a new teacher, serve as a peer coach, and make a difference in the lives of other teachers by serving as a positive role model.

Why is teacher leadership especially important at the elementary level? This question begs for an answer. First, the work of elementary teachers is key to a child's development. Dodge, Jablon, and Bickart (1994) assert that, "the early childhood and elementary school years establish a foundation for life-long learning. Therefore, *how* teachers guide children's learning is as important as *what* children are learning" (p. 139, emphasis in the original). Second, there are many aspects of an elementary curriculum that are developmental—that parallel the developmental stages of young children. It is at this level that children are socialized to school, continue to learn how to interact with peers and adults, and learn many of the fundamental skills that will follow them through life—reading, writing, and the ability to solve problems.

Just as a solid curricular foundation across the content areas sets the stage for learning in the middle and high schools, active parent participation during the early elementary years provides a foundation for more dynamic partnerships with parents throughout middle and high school. Teacher leadership in the elementary grades will have varying structures, depending on the local school. Although formal leadership opportunities in the elementary schools carry many labels, this chapter examines two teacher leadership structures: the grade level leader and the teacher facilitator.

Partnerships with Parents

Perhaps the most important partnership that a school can forge is with parents. Involving parents in the education process from early childhood can help nurture in students and parents a healthy attitude toward learning. Parents can be strong allies in assisting school personnel with finding solutions to behavioral issues and by making informed student placement decisions. More importantly, however, a strong start in the building of positive parent–school relationships can help pave the way for the types of relationships that teachers in later grades need to be able to foster with parents. Teacher leaders at the elementary level are in an advantageous position to help students and their parents to have a solid beginning in school.

Dealing with parents can be either enjoyable or frustrating, or both, for teachers. The teacher leader can do much in the way of preventing frustration and promoting cooperation by offering advice, guidelines, and strategies for building relationships with parents. The most important aspect of dealing with parents is communication. Communication on several different levels will go a long way toward creating an atmosphere of greater understanding and respect for the parent as well as the work teachers do to help students.

Parent–teacher conferences provide an important forum for teachers to develop a relationship with the family unit and school. Many districts provide from two to four days (or nights) during the school year for teachers and parents to interact with one another. The teacher leader can help other teachers through this process by modeling proactive behaviors and by providing guidelines for dealing with parents.

An excellent professional development activity that can help the teacher leader model effective parent–teacher interaction is to perform role-plays during a faculty meeting immediately before formal parent–teacher conferences.

This type of learning can increase the likelihood that the faculty—both new and veteran teachers—and administrators will be prepared to welcome parents to their child's school. Participants in such role-play activities can assume the role of the parent, teacher, administrator, and even student.

What types of parent–teacher conferences should be modeled during this inservice? Examples might include: the perfect conference, the angry parent conference, the conference where the student is present, and the poorly-planned-for conference. Each of these types of conferences is one that teachers might encounter. Observing and participating in these activities will make the information come alive, motivate teachers, increase teacher confidence, and promote empathy for the work and role parents play in their children's education. If teacher leaders organize and participate in this staff development, while simultaneously including teachers, administrators, and a student or two, the impact will be much greater for fellow faculty members.

Another strategy that the teacher leader can use to aid in parent conferences is developing a list of guidelines and suggestions obtained from veteran teachers and administrators. Putting these suggestions in an organized and to-the-point format to which teachers can quickly refer will make the suggestions more accessible. Figure 3.1 includes some suggestions that the teacher leader might pass along for the preparation for parent–teacher conferences.

Figure 3.1. Tips for Parent Teacher Conferences

- Prepare your classroom with student work and information about class expectations, homework policies, and class rules.
- Have an organized and clean space for conferencing—show that you care.
- Provide an area for parents who are waiting, and furnish the waiting parents with information about your subject area, class activities, or program.
- Consider a short video presentation concentrating on the students for those in the waiting area.
- Provide comfortable seating.
- Sit next to parents. Do not hide or intimidate from behind the desk.
- Be sure to have handbooks, information sheets, and policies (attendance, discipline and grading) readily accessible.
- Be certain to have grade information (books or computer printouts), test scores, behavior data, and general and specific written comments available.
- Approach conferences with a positive attitude—remember, "Parents love their children."

Teacher leaders can also help by offering strategies for use during a conference, and Figure 3.2 provides some sample strategies.

Figure 3.2. Strategies for Parent–Teacher Conferences

- Be prepared through prior planning.
- Be on time.
- Greet each parent naturally.
- Begin each conference on a positive note.
- Be a caring listener; show parents that they have your full attention.
- Speak clearly and precisely, but not too formally. Do not talk "down" to parents.
- Discover the needs of the parents and respond in a genuine manner.
- Do not get defensive or personally critical of a child or parent.
- Offer documentation to back up the positive or not so positive information that you share.
- Summarize key points at the end of the conference.
- Try to end on a positive note and offer to schedule a future conference if time runs out.

A newsletter can be another effective way to communicate with parents. Parent volunteers can assist in the production process, in either formatting the letter itself, writing a column, or folding, stamping, and mailing the newsletters.

Although almost every parent will have had prior experience in schools, parents will probably have selective memories, both on the positive and negative side about their schooling. Teacher leaders can help to create a "real-world" view of today's educational environment by organizing parent participation in school activities. Parents can assist with in-school and out-of-school activities, and they can provide invaluable help with school parties and celebrations, fund-raising events, and even duties and classroom projects.

The school-wide, departmental, or grade level teacher leader can be the focal point in weaving parents into the fabric of the school. Teacher leaders can participate in the process of determining the "best fit" for individual parents in appropriate roles within the school. Working directly with parents on committees, in the parent–teacher organization, or through other types of parent groups affords teachers with opportunities to forge new and stronger relationships with parents.

Often, teacher leaders and administrators deal with angry parents. The role of the leader in the situation where a fellow teacher may potentially be under "attack" from a parent is one of providing support and guidance. Conferences with angry or emotional parents need to be witnessed by an additional party. Some teachers are uncomfortable asking an administrator to attend, and, practically speaking, the teacher leader may have a clearer picture of the situation and be more familiar with the parent(s). The teacher leader may provide cues to the teacher, clarify and calm the situation, and, if necessary, end the conference with the promise to bring in administrators or other professionals in a future meeting. The role of the teacher leader, in this instance, is that of protecting the teacher—a valuable role that is sometimes overlooked even by the teachers involved in the process.

Curriculum Alignment and Vertical Teaming

As elementary teachers work to involve parents, they also provide the curricular foundation for student learning. As state and national mandates continue to raise the bar of accountability, schools are becoming increasingly aware of the need for a carefully aligned curriculum across the PK–12 continuum. Because of teacher leaders' expertise and, in response to increasing accountability, some districts are depending more on teachers to become experts and leaders in the schools, at the district level, and on state-level curriculum committees.

Teacher leaders find themselves in the unique position of having eyes in the front and the back of their heads. Teacher leaders have the broader "big picture" viewpoint that goes beyond their own classrooms. To effectively lead in the process of aligning curriculum, the teacher leader first needs to examine the curriculum.

Curriculum Analysis

English (1984) asserts there are three curricula that exist within every school: (a) the real curriculum, (b) the written curriculum, and (c) the tested curriculum. The *real curriculum* is that which is taught. The taught curriculum can vary from teacher to teacher within any given department. For example, if there is more than one person teaching reading, the taught curriculum will probably not be identical from teacher to teacher. The *written curriculum* is the official curriculum found in district or site curriculum handbooks. The *tested curriculum* is the curriculum that is assessed through standardized testing, usually mandated by the states. Figure 3.3 illustrates the curricula as described by English. We provide a new dimension common to all three curricula: instruction.

Figure 3.3. An Overlapping Curriculum

Source: Zepeda, S. J., & Mayers, R. S. (2000) Supervision and Staff Development in the Block. Larchmont, NY: Eye On Education. Used with Permission.

The overlapping area of the curricula represents the extent to which the three align. The larger this area is, the more aligned a school's overall curriculum will be. Figure 3.4 depicts a highly aligned school curriculum.

Figure 3.4. Highly Aligned Curriculum

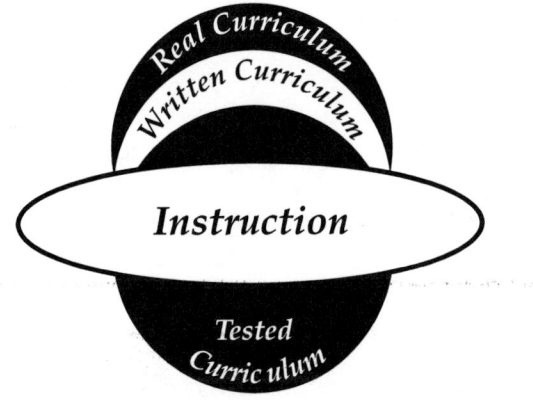

Source: Zepeda, S. J., & Mayers, R. S. (2000) Supervision and Staff Development in the Block. Larchmont, NY: Eye On Education. Used with Permission.

The area of alignment is, perhaps, most worth examining. In most districts, teachers spend countless hours developing the written curriculum and constructing curriculum guides. This process usually begins with the textbook adoption process.

As textbooks are being selected, learning objectives and goals (both local and state) are examined. During this examination process, teachers:

- Modify goals and objectives based on recency (when necessary);
- Select textbooks and other resources necessary to meet content goals; and,
- Refine district curriculum guides.

When these tasks (and perhaps others) are completed, the written curriculum is in place. The taught curriculum develops because of what teachers do in their classrooms, making subtle changes to adapt the written curriculum to the needs of students and the context of the classroom.

The critical area that links the real, written, and tested curricula is instructional strategies. By varying instructional strategies, teachers bring life to the curriculum, and this is one reason why it is important to develop instructional pacing guides.

The impact and effectiveness of the real and written curricula, coupled with the impact of instruction, is measured through the sphere of the tested curriculum. The tested curriculum occurs at multiple stages:

- Daily assessment associated with teaching (live interaction);
- Teacher-driven formal assessments, such as daily quizzes, chapter/unit tests, midterm/final examinations, presentations of portfolios, a mock trial, a reenactment of a major historical event, etc.; and,
- State-mandated tests.

Curriculum Alignment

"In-site" curriculum alignment occurs within the school. "Trans-site" alignment involves similar grade levels at different sites. Whatever form of curriculum alignment is used, there are a few important aspects for the teacher leader to consider in the process:

- Involve teachers from the beginning of the process to the "final" report.
- Use outside experts to evaluate existing curriculum and delivery systems.
- Have more than one method of evaluation.
- Make necessary adjustments within the process to increase or to maintain teacher "buy-in."

- Be very clear about the final product before mapping details or identifying skills.
- Make every effort to actively involve each grade level in the process.
- Include counselors, itinerant teachers, and paraprofessionals in the process, whenever possible.
- Be goal-oriented, but leave enough time during the process for reflection, related professional development seminars, and self-study (or group study).

Curriculum alignment can be a long process, but is an excellent opportunity for the teacher leader to do important work for students and faculty while developing working relationships with site and district administrators.

Vertical Teaming

Vertical teaming refers to the structuring of instructional methods and course content within a subject area at a site, or through one or more site levels (e.g., elementary school, middle school, and high school). Vertical teaming:

- Encourages articulation and communication between teachers of elementary, middle, and high school.
- Enables teachers to bridge the gap between elementary, middle, and high school by collaboration and communication.
- Helps teachers to coordinate and integrate curriculum and teacher/learning styles for all students.
- Includes all students.
- Can increase student confidence in thinking skills.
- Provides stronger instructional cohesion and sequential development of skills and knowledge.
- Incorporates instructional methodologies that provoke a stronger inductive approach to teaching and emphasizes greater student responsibility for learning.
- Provides opportunities for elementary, middle, and high school teachers to meet and discuss common areas of curriculum and pedagogy.
- Establishes a network for parent participation in the program.
- Gives teachers the satisfaction of knowing that their students will be continuing their education in a program that they have helped to

personally develop along with other teachers in the vertical team. (Plano Independent School District)

Vertical teams are comprised of one teacher leader per grade level or site level, and team membership can range in number from 7 to 14 members. Success for the school or district is dependent on the cooperation and collaboration of the teacher leaders who represent many faculty members in the process of vertical teaming. The work of the vertical team is to produce a visual picture that represents the skills and content of a specified curriculum (content and subject area) from one level or grade to the next. Figure 3.5 depicts a spiraled curriculum.

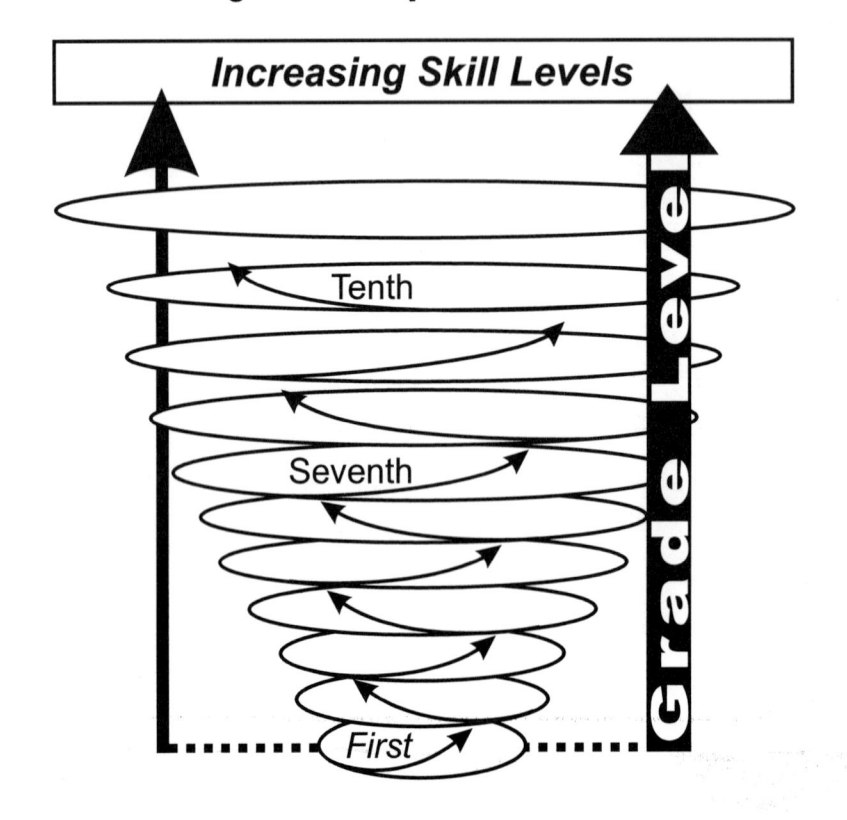

Figure 3.5. A Spiral Curriculum

Each leader's voice is equally important, and each is necessary to create a comprehensive and coordinated program within a subject area whether it is across the school or the entire district.

If one teacher leader is spearheading the process at a site or for the entire team, there are a few things to keep in mind to keep the work of the team moving toward the result, examining the curricular program. Figure 3.6 provides some direction for keeping the work of vertical teams moving across grade levels.

Figure 3.6. Considerations to Keep Vertical Teams Spiraling Across Grade Levels

- Teams should include one leader from each grade level.
- Size of teams may range from 7 to 14 members. If more representation is needed in an area or grade level, the team leader should consider splitting the teams and tasks.
- Prepare updates and progress reports for the entire faculty.
- Value equally each teacher leader's knowledge.
- Consider traveling to other districts that use the vertical teaming model.
- Attend workshops or seminars on the vertical teaming process.

Vertical teaming can also take on a more literal meaning. In many districts, programs such as band, orchestra, and choir employ team teaching across sites and across grade levels. Vertical teaming provides an opportunity to extend and promote:

- Informal supervision.
- Multi-site action research projects.
- A deeper understanding of the appropriateness of curriculum for a specific level.
- A complete view of the learning "string."
- A stronger sense of purpose for the main teaching assignment.
- An almost immediate as well as an ongoing opportunity for assessment.
- The sharing of creative ideas with other professionals.

Regardless of the form the vertical teaming process takes, teacher leaders, as the major figures in the process, have the opportunity to transform schools and their systems.

The Work of Grade Level Leaders

In many elementary schools, teacher leadership takes the form of grade level leaders. Stone, Horejs, and Lomas (1997) found that elementary teachers view accomplishments in terms of grade level rather than as school-wide accomplishments. Grade level leaders are instructional leaders, and Figure 3.7 provides a sample grade level leader job description.

Figure 3.7. Grade Level Leader Job Description

- Serve as a liaison between grade level teachers and administration.
- Write duty schedule (early morning, recess, lunch room, afternoon pick up) for grade level teachers.
- Coordinate grade level gifted and talented enrichment activities.
- Conduct regular grade level meetings.
- Coordinate parental paperwork for field trips.
- Write grants to purchase instructional supplies (math manipulatives, materials for gifted and talented activities).
- Coordinate textbook adoption and ordering.
- Coordinate parental communications (e.g., open houses, special events).
- Prepare required supply list (e.g., pencils, paper, crayons) for posting at area retail stores.
- Work with local businesses to secure student awards (e.g., reading initiatives).
- Assist with the induction and mentoring of new teachers.

Used by permission of DeQueen Primary School, DeQueen, Arkansas.

As with high school department and middle school team meetings, grade level meetings are most effective when not used as an oral memo. Grade level meetings need to be spent discussing student, curricular, teaching, and learning issues. Figure 3.8 gives an example of a meeting agenda.

Figure 3.8. Sample Grade Level Meeting Agenda

Grade 2 Meeting Agenda
March 25, 2002   3:30 to 4:45 P.M.   Room 109

- Student issues
- Curricular issues
- Staff development needs
- Announcements
- Upcoming special events
- Open discussion
- Adjourn

Grade level meetings normally address three major areas: (a) student learning issues, (b) professional development for teachers, and (c) housekeeping items. Effective grade level meetings emphasize student and teacher learning.

Elementary teachers spend more of the day with the same students than do secondary teachers. Moreover, elementary teachers instruct and assess students over a wider range of academic disciplines than do secondary teachers. For these reasons, elementary teachers are in a more advantageous position to gain a broader view of each student's academic progress by collecting data on each student across multiple disciplines. Grade level meetings provide an excellent forum for sharing student data and making informed decisions based on that data.

A discussion of strategies for improving student learning should also be a part of grade level meetings. These discussions should include how to:

- Make the best use of paraprofessionals and teacher aides to extend the efforts of the classroom teacher;

- Involve parents both at school and at home to support student learning; and,

- Create relevant, appropriate professional development opportunities available to grade level teachers to continue their learning.

Only when the connection between teacher learning and student learning is made will teachers be in a position to model lifelong learning for their students.

Coordinating the Work of Teachers across Grade Levels

Although many elementary schools use grade level leaders to coordinate instruction and activities with specific grades, teacher leadership across grade levels is also important. Primary to this reason is that children experience greater development in more areas (physical, language acquisition, and cognitive—especially concrete problem-solving skills and emotional development) during the elementary years than at any other time (Woolfolk, 1993). Among the tasks needing attention across grade levels are monitoring vertical alignment of the curriculum and maintaining classroom management policies.

Monitoring Vertical Alignment of the Curriculum

The acquisition of language and problem-solving skills in the elementary grades provides a necessary foundation for the learning that students are expected to accomplish in middle and high school. According to Dodge, Jablon, and Bickart (1994), these skills include "language and literacy, mathematical thinking, scientific thinking, social inquiry, and the ability to express their ideas through the arts and technology" (p. 3). By closely monitoring the curriculum from a vertical perspective, elementary educators can help ensure that all students are taught needed basic skills.

Grade level leaders are well situated to coordinate curriculum across grade levels. Strategies that can assist in vertically aligning the curriculum include:

- Meeting with other grade level leaders to stay informed about curricular developments in other grades;
- Conducting cross-grade-level meetings so teachers in different grades can coordinate what they teach and how; and
- Using paraprofessionals or teacher aides to create release time for teachers to observe one another.

Maintaining Consistent Classroom Discipline Policies

According to Katz and Chard (1989), it is during the elementary years that children need to develop "the dispositions to be a learner—curiosity, independence, responsibility, initiative, creativity, willingness to take risks, to ask questions, and to persevere" (p. 30). By maintaining consistent classroom management policies across classrooms and grade levels, elementary educators create an environment that supports curiosity, creativity, risk taking, and inquisitiveness that are hallmarks of learning. Consistent classroom management strategies across classrooms also offer students added reinforcement of the social skills necessary for a productive learning environment.

A Case Study from the Field: DeQueen Primary School, DeQueen, Arkansas

> *Curricular Leadership: A Reading Initiative*
> DeQueen Primary School
> Lynda Beltrani, Principal
> Treating Plant Road, DeQueen, AR 71832
> 870-642-3100
> Fax: 870-642-7360
> E-mail: lbeltran@leopards.k12.ar.us
> Online: www.leopards.k12.ar.us
> DeQueen Public Schools
> Mr. Bill Blackwood, Superintendent

DeQueen Primary School, a rural school situated in southwest Arkansas, is comprised of grades K–2 and enrolls approximately 525 students. Principal

Lynda Beltrani and Assistant Principal Sharon Dykes work with a staff of 32 teachers, 14 paraprofessionals, and 1 counselor. The population is largely a mix of white and Hispanic students.

Teacher leadership is an expectation at DeQueen Primary School as evidenced by three groups of teacher leaders: (a) grade level leaders, (b) "Smart Start" facilitators, and (c) Cadre Persons. Grade level leaders support instructional efforts within grade levels, "Smart Start" facilitators are staff developers for teachers within the framework of a statewide initiative, and Cadre Persons are peer coaches and program evaluators with specific responsibility for reading achievement.

Grade Level Leaders at DeQueen Primary School

Grade level leaders at DeQueen Primary School are responsible for supporting instruction within their grade levels (see Figure 3.7 for a job description).

The tasks of these teacher leaders focus on:

- Ensuring that all teachers within their grade level have sufficient instructional supplies.
- Writing grants to fund grade level initiatives.
- Acting as a communication liaison between the grade level teachers and the administrators.

Grade level leaders are also the frontline support for all teachers new to DeQueen Primary School, whether veteran or novice. Inducting and mentoring new teachers is an important part of the process of building the learning community at DeQueen Primary School.

The work of the grade level leaders is supported by the administration through release time. Instead of specific hours set aside for grade level work, release time for grade level leaders is created as needed with substitute teachers and paraprofessionals. Regular meetings with the grade level leaders assist the principal and assistant principal to keep abreast of grade level initiatives and to support grade level work.

Smart Start Facilitators

Smart Start is an initiative supported by the Arkansas State Department of Education that seeks to increase student learning by more closely aligning the curriculum, instruction, and student assessment. An important part of Smart Start is supporting student learning by increasing the opportunities available for teachers to learn. In sum, Smart Start facilitators are staff developers.

DeQueen Primary has two Smart Start facilitators, and their job description is provided in Figure 3.9.

Figure 3.9. Job Description for Smart Start Facilitators

Smart Start Facilitators:
- Attend statewide staff development for Smart Start Facilitators.
- Conduct staff development functions at the site.
- Establish learning teams at the site.
- Assist in the development of site instructional plans.
- Facilitate and support adult learning between formal staff development events.
- Support teachers as they learn to integrate new skills into their practices.
- Encourage dialogue among teachers.
- Provide opportunities for reflection and for teacher to evaluate their teaching.
- Foster an environment conducive to change.

Used with permission of DeQueen Primary School, DeQueen, Arkansas.

To support the work of the Smart Start facilitators, DeQueen Primary School funds facilitators' participation in statewide staff development opportunities, provides access to current research on teaching and learning, and assists with facilitators' efforts to network with staff developers statewide and nationwide.

Cadre Persons and the Direct Instruction Coordinator

Through program evaluation efforts conducted during the 1995–1996 school year by teachers and administrators at DeQueen Primary School, low reading ability among students was identified as the major cause of declining standardized test scores. After researching alternatives for raising reading achievement, teachers and administrators chose to implement a program called Direct Instruction (DI). Direct Instruction, supported by an out-of-state consultant, is reading instruction delivered to students who are grouped by ability.

The first step in implementing the DI program was for DeQueen teachers to visit other schools that were using the program. Following site visits, teachers participated in an intensive, one-week staff development inservice conducted by the outside consultant. To provide for the ongoing teacher learning needs to support the DI program, a corps of teacher leaders were recruited and trained.

The DI program is coordinated by a teacher leader (the Direct Instruction Coordinator) and supported by other teacher leaders called Cadre Persons. The DI Coordinator oversees the Direct Instruction Program. The DI Coordinator's job description is offered in Figure 3.10

Figure 3.10. Direct Instruction Coordinator's Job Description

Direct Instruction Coordinators:
- Ensure all teachers have needed supplies.
- Coordinate periodic visits by the outside consultant.
- Coordinate program evaluation efforts and provide written feedback to teachers.
- Oversee student assessment schedule.
- Assists in formulating student groups.
- Maintain student placement and assessment records.
- Assist teachers to develop pacing guides.
- Analyze lesson plans and pacing with Cadre Leaders.
- Support needed ongoing staff development for Cadre Leaders and teachers.

Used with permission of DeQueen Primary School, DeQueen, Arkansas.

The cadre persons are the teacher leaders who provide the first line of support for the Direct Instruction Reading Initiative. Each grade level has one cadre person. Cadre persons have the following responsibilities:

- Coach teachers within their grade level.
- Collect data from groups within their grade level for use in conducting program evaluation.
- Assist grade level teachers to create remediation plans where needed.
- Help to identify students who need to be transferred to a different group.
- Work with the DI Coordinator to conduct ongoing program evaluation.
- Act as a liaison between grade level teachers and the DI Coordinator.

The DI program has been in place at DeQueen Primary School for five years. Data collected (DI student assessments, standardized test scores) and analyzed as part of the ongoing program evaluation indicate a significant increase in student reading achievement.

The Work of a Teacher Facilitator

In some elementary schools, formal teacher leadership takes the form of a teacher facilitator. A teacher facilitator is a coach, confidant, staff developer, and communicator. Figure 3.11 depicts a sample organizational chart of an elementary school with a teacher facilitator.

Figure 3.11. Teacher Facilitator Organizational Chart

```
                    Principal
                        |
                        v
                Assistant Principal
            /           |           \
           v            v            v
    Counselor   Teacher Facilitator   Media Specialist
                /     |     |     \
               v      v     v      v
           PK Team  Kindergarten  1st Grade  2nd Grade
                       Team        Team       Team
```

Teacher facilitators can be the sole formal teacher leadership position, or they can work in concert with grade level leaders. The many names that school systems use for referring to their teacher leaders are not as important as the work that they accomplish. Regardless of which title is used, teacher facilitators are well situated to be instructional leaders, staff developers, and an important hub in the elementary school's communication network. For a fuller discussion of the teacher facilitator, the reader is encouraged to examine the case study of Gunter Elementary School offered at the end of this chapter.

The Unique Relationship between a Teacher Facilitator and the Principal

Similar to a middle school instructional lead teacher, the elementary teacher facilitator has a unique relationship with the principal. The teacher facilitator works closely with the principal. The work of a teacher facilitator includes curriculum alignment, staff development, and parent involvement.

It is important to realize that the elementary teacher facilitator is not an administrator but is, instead, a *teacher* leader. Perhaps most importantly, teacher facilitators supervise teachers, but in different ways—they conduct classroom observations, coach teachers, teach demonstration lessons, and create connections to staff development. However, they do not evaluate teachers. Because evaluation is connected to employment decisions, it is solely within the purview of the principal or an assistant principal. So, what is the relationship between the teacher facilitator and the principal?

The teacher facilitator is a confidant and a coach for teachers and, at the same time, a close coworker of the principal. Key to managing the tension between these two roles is maintaining a high level of trust between the teacher facilitator and the teachers as well as between the teacher facilitator and the principal. A teacher facilitator cannot function as a confidant to teachers if the facilitator is viewed as an informant for the principal. At the same time, the principal must respect the teacher facilitator's need to conduct confidential conversations behind the office door and to trust that these meetings are constructive learning opportunities and not destructive gripe sessions.

A Case Study from the Field: Teacher Leadership at Gunter Elementary School, Gunter, Texas

A Vision of Teacher Leadership

Gunter Elementary School
Cheyrl A. Cohagan, Principal
Dara Arrington, Teacher Facilitator
100 W. Pecan, Gunter, TX 75058
903-433-5315
Fax: 903-433-1184
E-mail: ccohagan@gunterisd.org
E-mail: darrrington@gunterisd.org
Online: www.gunterisd.org
Gunter Independent School District
Richard W. Cohagan, Superintendent

The following case study explores teacher leadership and is an example of the potential that teacher leadership can have in a school system. Teachers are leaders when they "fill the gap" in assisting schools, and their people grow and develop.

A Vision of Teacher Leadership

Gunter Elementary School is located in Gunter, Texas, a town just north of the Dallas-Fort Worth metropolitan area. Principal Cheyrl Cohagan works with 20 teachers and 2 teacher aides to serve an enrollment of 240 students in prekindergarten through the fourth grade. At Gunter Elementary, all teachers are expected to be leaders. The philosophy that undergirds teaching and learning at Gunter Elementary has two components:

1. Everyone in the school is a learner.
2. Teacher learning is prerequisite to student learning.

According to Ms. Cohagan, teachers who are active learners are also leaders—the two are inseparable.

Teacher Leadership at Gunter Elementary

At Gunter Elementary School, few formal leadership titles such as grade level leader are used. However, teachers within each grade level are expected to make decisions concerning grade level and school-wide initiatives in the areas of staff development, curriculum alignment, and instructional practices. In addition, teachers are also expected to take charge of their individual learning needs. Forums such as grade level meetings and general faculty meetings are viewed as staff development opportunities, not as "verbal memos."

Grade level meetings at Gunter Elementary School have three major purposes: (a) to plan instruction, (b) to make decisions concerning staff development needs, and (c) to set grade level goals that support school and district goals. Team planning assists the Gunter faculty by:

- Ensuring all students are exposed to the same curriculum and are learning the same skills.
- Providing the faculty with a weekly forum to discuss problems of practice,
- Supporting faculty efforts to work as a team.

Weekly faculty meetings are viewed as opportunities to plan formal staff development, for teachers to engage colleagues in discussion about classroom concerns, and as an important opportunity for Gunter's teachers to participate in making school-wide decisions. In response to legislation raising the bar of accountability for reading achievement, there was the need to increase capacity for supporting teacher learning at Gunter Elementary. The solution became known as the teacher facilitator.

The Teacher Facilitator at Gunter Elementary School

Introduced for the 2001–2002 school year, a veteran teacher, Ms. Dara Arrington, became the teacher facilitator for Gunter Elementary School. To emphasize that the teacher facilitator is a *teacher* leadership position, as opposed to an administrative one, Ms. Arrington was provided an office well removed from the main office. It was important to the principal that the teacher facilitator be viewed as a teacher leader and not as an assistant principal. Because the position is new, a formal job description is still under construction, and Figure 3.12 provides a profile of the work of the teacher facilitator.

Figure 3.12. The Work of the Teacher Facilitator

The Teacher Facilitator:
- Conducts classroom observations.
- Coaches teachers.
- Reviews current research and provides relevant readings to teachers.
- Coordinates formal staff development events.
- Meets with grade levels to facilitate discussion of instructional issues and to support team-building efforts.
- Works as a liaison between grade levels.
- Assists with program evaluation.
- Models best practices in teaching.
- Teaches classes to create release time for teachers.
- Serves as a liaison between the teaching faculty and principal.
- Helps teachers to set goals consistent with site and district goals.

Used with Permission of Gunter Elementary School, Gunter, Texas.

An examination of the work of the teacher facilitator demonstrates the focus on teacher growth and instructional improvement. This work has three streams: (a) instructional leadership, (b) staff developer, and (c) communicator.

The Teacher Facilitator as an Instructional Leader

According to Ms. Arrington, much of her work takes place in teachers' classrooms. At least five benefits are derived from these classroom observations. These include:

- Increasing teacher comfort with an observer in the classroom
- Assisting the teacher facilitator to become familiar with each teachers' strengths and areas where growth may be needed
- Providing opportunities for teachers to receive increased feedback about growth areas
- Helping the teacher facilitator to increase teacher dialogue across grade levels by sharing good things that are happening in classrooms
- Enabling the teacher facilitator to identify teacher expertise that can be used to support staff development efforts.

Being a regular observer in classrooms opens other avenues for teacher facilitator to support the work of teachers. These opportunities include being a teacher coach and sharing observed innovative teaching strategies with teachers in other grade levels. The presence of the teacher facilitator in classrooms also supports the role as a staff developer, and this presence helps the teacher facilitator share best practices with even more teachers.

The Teacher Facilitator as a Staff Developer

Another key role of the teacher facilitator at Gunter Elementary School is that of staff developer. Informal classroom observations provide a bird's-eye view of teaching, and this information assists the teacher facilitator to identify staff development needs and to locate potential staff developers among the teachers. As staff development needs are identified, strategies for meeting those needs are identified at grade level meetings and at faculty meetings.

As the teacher facilitator, Ms. Arrington works with the principal to provide the conditions necessary (release time, outside facilitators) for staff development for teachers. Important to launching the efforts of the new teacher facilitator, Principal Cohagan became Ms. Arrington's staff developer. This staff development included mentoring in the skills necessary to work with teachers, visits to other schools to observe other administrators working with teachers, and opportunities for Ms. Arrington to discuss the meaning of her working with teachers.

Teacher Facilitator as Communicator

The third stream in the teacher facilitator's work is fostering communication—within grade levels, between levels, and between the teachers and the principal. As new teachers are hired, the teacher facilitator works with these teachers to assist them in learning the culture and expectations of Gunter Elementary School. Through induction and mentoring, the teacher facilitator supports new teachers in becoming a part of their grade level team.

A necessary condition for team building is to create an atmosphere of trust where teachers can discuss instructional issues knowing that their openness will not be used against them. As a teacher facilitator, Ms. Arrington provides the teachers of Gunter Elementary School a "safe place" to vent frustrations and to get help. By working as a communication link between the teachers and the principal, the teacher facilitator has provided the Gunter faculty with multiple options for expressing concerns and seeking assistance. Multiple communication channels provide multiple sources for supporting teachers and their learning.

Teacher Leadership Creates Powerful Learning Opportunities for Teachers

Creating a full-time teacher leadership position (the teacher facilitator) has proven to be an important step in increasing the learning capacity of all teachers at Gunter Elementary School. However, real learning capacity for individual teachers increases only when teachers are given the power to make decisions about their own learning. The source of this power is the principal. As demonstrated by Gunter Elementary School's learning community, teacher leadership is the result of empowerment and active learning, not the granting of titles.

Chapter Summary

At the elementary level, students learn the language, mathematical, inquiry, and thinking skills—and they develop the dispositions (curiosity, independnce, and responsibility)—that can support them as learners all their lives. For this important learning to occur, elementary teachers need to be active learners. This learning is best supported through the work of teacher leaders such as grade level leaders, teacher facilitators, or both. Teachers who are empowered are active learners—they examine their practices for areas to improve and then search for professional growth opportunities that will support the learning necessary for that instructional improvement to occur.

References

Dodge, D. T., Jablon, J. R., & Bickart, T. S. (1994). *Constructing curriculum for the primary grades.* Washington, DC: Teaching Strategies.

English, F. (1984). Curriculum mapping and management. In B. D. Sattes (Ed.), *Promoting school excellence through the application of effective schools research: Summary and proceedings of a 1984 regional exchange workshop.* (ERIC Document Reproduction Service No. ED251972)

Katz, L., & Chard, S. (1989). *Engaging children's minds: The project approach.* Norwood, NJ: Ablex.

Plano Independent School District. *Team teaching.* Retrieved June 29, 2002, from http://www.pisd.edu/AOS/General/teamteac.htm#vertical

Stone, M., Horejs, J., & Lomas, A. (1997, March). *Commonalities and differences in teacher leadership at the elementary, middle, and high school levels.* Paper presented at the annual meeting of the American Educational Research Association, Chicago.

Woolfolk, A. E. (1993). *Educational psychology* (5th ed.). Needham Heights, MA: Allyn & Bacon.

Zepeda, S. J., & Mayers, R. S. (2000). *Supervision and staff development in the block.* Larchmont, NY: Eye On Education.

4

Teacher Leadership in the Middle Grades

In this Chapter

- The Instructional Lead Teacher
- Getting Started as an Instructional Lead Teacher—Learning the Ropes
- The Instructional Lead Teacher in the "Middle" of Management
- School Governance and Teacher Leadership in the Middle School
- Duties and Responsibilities of the Instructional Lead Teacher
- The Middle School Team Leader
- Duties and Issues for the Team Leader

Introducing Teacher Leadership in the Middle Grades

The inclusion of grades in middle-level schools varies. The junior high model (grades 7–9) was the most prevalent through the mid 1970s, but middle schools (grades 6–8) now outnumber the junior high configuration. One of the defining beliefs of middle school thought is that the social and emotional development of the middle school student is an important part of supporting academic achievement. Areas of study (e.g., music, art, shop, home economics, and technology) that fall outside of content areas (e.g., math, science, English) are also important. Opportunities for teacher leadership—instructional lead teachers and team leaders—abound in the middle school.

The Instructional Lead Teacher (ILT)

The middle school instructional lead teacher (ILT) is a locally defined leadership position. In general, the ILT receives release from teaching duties (either full-time or part-time) to assist teachers with instruction, to monitor the implementation of the district's curricular objectives, to conduct informal classroom observations to support instructional improvement, and to work with the principal (and perhaps assistant principals and deans) to support the instructional program. Consider the following configuration of the typical middle school as indicated in Figure 4.1.

Figure 4.1. The Relationship of the Middle School ILT to Teachers and Administrators

```
                          Principal
              ┌──────────────┼──────────────┐
              ▼              ▼              ▼
     Assistant Principal  Assistant Principal  Assistant Principal
              └──────────────┼──────────────┘
                             ▼
                      Instructional
                      Lead Teacher
              ┌──────────┬────┴─────┬──────────┐
              ▼          ▼          ▼          ▼
           Team       Team        Team        Team
          Leader     Leader      Leader      Leader
            │          │           │           │
            ▼          ▼           ▼           ▼
           Team       Team        Team        Team
         Members    Members     Members     Members
        (Teachers) (Teachers)  (Teachers)  (Teachers)
```

From Figure 4.1, it can be seen that the ILT is in the "middle" of the school structure. The work of the instructional lead teacher is important to both grade level teams and the administrative team. What types of work does an ILT do? A sample ILT job description (Figure 4.2) portrays the type of work and the myriad tasks that the ILT performs to assist teams school personnel.

Figure 4.2. Sample Instructional Lead Teacher Job Description

Duties and Responsibilities: Instructional Lead Teacher

- Prepare and coordinate school reports/grants.
- Coordinate parent involvement initiatives.
- Monitor field trips and video requests.
- Serve on the school's leadership team as a permanent member along with the principal and assistant principals.
- Attend all faculty meetings, PTO (Parent–Teacher Organization) meetings and any and all meetings assigned by the principal.
- Coordinate the duties and the responsibilities of the team leaders.
  - meeting times (one meeting per month should deal with school improvement/staff development)
  - minutes
  - activities
- Assist the staff development contact person with the direction of the staff development program and school improvement plan.
- Consult with teachers in the selection and evaluation of textbooks and materials.
- Coordinate site-based curriculum alignment.
- Consult with teachers to plan instructional strategies for students who are performing below grade level.
- Coordinate curriculum areas in conjunction with team leaders.
- Develop demonstration lessons and model appropriate teaching.
- Maintain and submit a weekly calendar to the principal.
- Conduct classroom observations.
- Any other duties assigned by the principal (including reading and evaluating lesson plans).

Used with permission, Griffin-Spalding Public Schools, Griffin, Georgia.

ILTs work alongside the administrative team and teams of teachers; hence, the ILT has "one foot" in the work of teaching and the "other foot" in the work of administration.

Getting Started as an Instructional Lead Teacher—Learning the Ropes

An ILT can learn the ropes through a variety of approaches that include networking with other district ILTs, surveying team leaders, and meeting frequently with the principal and other members of the administrative team. The new ILT needs to avail herself of as many sources of information as possible during the first year in the position. Artifacts such as a job description, faculty handbook, and other documents will provide insight for the ILT.

Network with Other ILTs in the District

The ILTs from the other middle schools in the district can provide mentoring for the new ILT. It is important to gain understanding of the history of why things are done the way they are. No two schools are the same, and even middle schools in the same system will do things differently. Therefore, the new ILT should always "think back" to the home school.

Meet with the Team Leaders

It is important to build bridges with grade level leaders and the teams they lead. Grade levels configure in teams, which are usually comprised of language arts, math, social studies, and science teachers with exploratory teachers complementing this structure. Teams enjoy latitude in arranging their "own schedules" for the day, week, month, or any other part of the school year, and this type of configuration promotes flexible scheduling—another defining feature of the middle school.

Each team has its own "leader" that works closely with the ILT. An added feature of flexible scheduling is that teams of teachers have built-in team meeting time—mostly on a daily basis. This is a time for teachers to plan for upcoming instruction (interdisciplinary units), to meet with the school counselor and other support staff (school psychologist, social worker) to devise strategies to work with students, and to complete work (progress reports). Often, the ILT attends team meetings and uses this time to communicate school-wide information while lending support to the work of teams.

For new ILTs, a meeting with team leaders and the use of a survey (such as the one presented in Figure 4.3) can help the ILT to determine the types of assistance needed.

Figure 4.3. Team Leader Survey

Dear Team Leaders:

As the new ILT, I need to know how I can support the work that you do as a team leader. Please reflect on the following and return this survey to me before we meet as a group next week. You might want to discuss the items on this survey with your team members—if you would like to complete this survey as a group, that would be great. I look forward to our work together this year, and, our principal, Mr. Martin, is committed to the ILT position being that of support provider. I share this vision.

Meg Demitri

Team: _____ (optional)

- How often should the ILT attend team meetings?

- Identify the goals you and your team have for the year.

  How can I support you and the team in achieving these goals?

- Indicate the support I can provide for the work of the team with regard to:

  - textbook adoption:

  - curriculum alignment:

  - development of interdisciplinary and thematic units:

  - staff development in specified areas (please specify needs):

  - standardized test preparation:

  - content standards and learning objectives:

  - team assemblies:

  - other:

- Last year, the ILT, team leaders, and administrators met once a week.

  - How often should the administrative team and team leaders meet?

  - Should we meet before or after school?

  - How can we better develop meeting agendas?

If you would like to add any other information, please use the back side of this survey. Again, I appreciate the time and effort taken to complete this survey.

The results from this survey place the ILT in a solid position to carve out ways to support teams. To keep communication channels open, the ILT should share survey results with the principal and the grade level leaders.

Provide Opportunities to Expand Interaction between and among Teams

School-wide issues need input from all stakeholders, and opportunities for teachers to meet according to subject area content (e.g., math, science, English) and across grade levels can be arranged by the ILT. A schedule that allows each grade level to meet once a month can be helpful. During the first month of school, the ILT can develop, in conjunction with the administrative team and team leaders, a master calendar of meetings.

The work of the ILT includes meeting individually with teachers, engaging in peer coaching, teaching demonstration lessons, and a host of other work related to the improvement of the instructional program. Visibility enhances credibility and helps to build relationships with teachers.

Credibility and Trust

The ILT is a teacher support specialist, and, in this capacity, serves as the liaison between the principal and team leaders. Given this position "in the middle," effective communication skills are essential. However, more important is credibility—the ILT needs to be credible in the eyes of both teachers and administrators. Trust is essential because the ILT is constantly communicating with teachers, administrators, parents, and the many constituencies found in schools. Trust between the principal and the ILT is important to the success of this position, and helps to set the conditions for the trust shared by the ILT and the teachers she works with. Careful attention to, and constant development of, trusting relationships will greatly enhance the effectiveness of the ILT.

Objectivity

The ILT is a sounding board for teachers and administrators, and the ILT may assume the role of being the "mirror" and the "window" for the administration and the faculty. Serving the dual role of faculty member and administrative liaison often allows ILTs to have a more complete perspective than either party. There may be times when the ILT can hold up the "mirror" to team leaders and teachers, so that they can view their practices more clearly and "see" what effect these practices may have on students. At other times, the ILT may be in a position to break down relational walls and encourage fellow educators to look through a "window" to see more clearly what each other may actually be thinking and doing, and what effect this may have on the school climate. This can encourage teachers and administrators to expand their sights from a "point of view" to a "viewing point."

Accountability, the Middle School Philosophy, and the Work of the Instructional Lead Teacher

Another aspect of the middle school environment that places the ILT squarely between opposing, albeit positive camps, is the almost perpetual tug of war in many schools between "student-centered" and "curriculum-centered" philosophies. With the advent of increased testing at the local, state, and national levels, the pull away from a student-centered curriculum is a reality felt by many middle school teachers and administrators. If these two philosophies are to coexist, the ILT needs to help maintain a balance between the emphasis on the student and on the curriculum. Middle school students need a blend of academic rigor and a nurturing environment.

To achieve this balance, the ILT needs to ascertain the current climate of the school and to nurture the beliefs of teachers. School-wide equilibrium will only occur when the "efforts" of the faculty and the administration, and the expectations of each other, align. The ILT is in a prime position to influence and maintain this balance.

A Case Study from the Field: School Governance and Teacher Leadership at Coile Middle School, Athens, Georgia

Shared Decision Making
W. R. Coile Middle School
Tim Jarboe, Principal
110 Old Elberton Road, Winterville, Georgia 30601
(706) 357-5318
FAX: (706) 357-5321
E-mail: jarboet@clarke.k12.ga.us
Online: www.clarke.k12.ga.us/coile
Clarke County School District
Dr. Lewis Holloway, Superintendent

Shared Decision Making

Principals affirm teachers when they empower them as decision makers. For teachers, having one's input requested, or, even more powerfully, *expected* in the decision-making process signals to teachers that their expertise and experience are *valued* and *needed*. Student issues, hiring decisions, and outreach initiatives all provide opportunities for teachers to become leaders and to stay in the classroom *at the same time.*

Coordinating decision making among teachers, staff members, and administrators requires negotiation and planning. Tim Jarboe, principal of Coile Middle School, describes the shared governance model in place in his school. Tim and his school have built a community that embraces shared decision making.

The School

Coile Middle School is one of four middle schools in the Clarke County School District, located in Winterville, Georgia—on the rural outskirts of Athens. The school consists of grades 6–8 with a student population of 650 students who are taught by 57 certificated staff members. Support personnel for teachers include a principal, assistant principal, instructional lead teacher, counselor, media specialist, and gifted facilitator.

Beginning Shared Governance

In 1995, the school district expanded from three to four middle schools, and Coile drew its student population and its certificated staff from the three existing middle schools. Before Coile Middle School opened, parents, students, and staff met to share ideas, concerns, and dreams for the *ideal* middle school. The following core values emerged:

- effective communication
- unity of purpose
- community of learners
- celebration
- nurturing/caring/compassionate environment
- high expectations
- responsibility and accountability
- orderly environment
- flexibility
- collaboration

Teacher Leadership in the Middle Grades

During the 1996-1997 school year, Coile began to move toward a shared-governance structure. After doing text-based research, looking at school accountability criteria, and viewing organizational models of shared governance at other schools, the current structure developed. As part of the commitment to shared governance, the entire staff serves on Action Teams and the Coile Congress (the decision-making body). As Coile has grown and changed, Mr. Jarboe, who before assuming the principalship served as Coile's Instructional Lead Teacher, reports that they continue to refine the process (Figure 4.4).

Figure 4.4. W. R. Coile Middle School Governance Structure

Coile Community Congress
(Where school-wide decisions are made)
All Coile staff members, any interested parents, community members, and students who are involved with an Action Team

Ad hoc Committees
Used for issues that do not "fit" an Action Team or need to be "fast-tracked."

Student Success Action Team
Intervention for students with special needs.

Communication Action Team
Creates and maintains a communication network between staff, students, parents/guardians, and community.

Steering Committee
- Makes sure recommendations of Action Teams align with the school vision.
- Serves as a communication vehicle for disseminating information to and from Action Teams, Coile Community Congress, and the principal.
- Decides whether issues go to actions teams, ad hoc committee, or to administration.
- Helps develop and refine recommendations to be presented to the Coile Community Congress for voting/consensus.

Evaluation Action Team
Collects, analyzes and summarizes data for program

Climate Action Team
Creates and maintains a safe, nurturing, and welcoming environment.

Administrative Decision
- May be made with input from teams/steering committee.
- May not involve input.

The Box
- Enables individuals to submit issues directly to Steering Committee.
- Issues must be signed.
- Student issues must be signed by a sponsor.

Curriculum and Instruction
Supports and maintains exemplary curriculum and innovation instruction.

Technology
Develops, implements, and provides staff development for the school-wide technology plan.

Evaluation of Effectiveness

The overall goal of Coile Middle School is to raise student achievement, and this goal, along with two subgoals, supports Coile's shared governance initiative by:

- Modeling for students a learning community where all members are part of the democratic process to make the community a better place.
- Fostering the strongest commitment possible from teachers to improve the learning environment by showing that their ideas and concerns shape the learning community.

Specific goals for student achievement, the materials needed, and the people responsible are set forth in Coile's annual School Improvement Plan. This plan sets goals for (a) student achievement in content areas, (b) technology, (c) improving instructional staff development, and (d) refining and involving more participants in the shared-governance structure. A specific Action Team, Content/Subject Area Team, or Instructional Support Person (i.e., principal, ILT) assumes responsibility for achieving the goals in the School Improvement Plan. Jarboe has the expectation that every staff member will be an active member of both an Action Team and a Content Area Team.

Resources and Support

The staff draws on local resources to support professional development needed for school improvement. Because the school's shared-governance system rests on the philosophy of enabling staff members to participate in the process based on their individual strengths, teacher expertise is the source for staff development. When expertise is unavailable within the school staff, professional development funds enable staff members to locate needed outside learning resources through professional travel, district/regional professional development courses, or the purchase of reference/research materials. The key to successfully using local resources lies in the manner in which the shared-governance process empowers teachers to make decisions regarding staff priorities. Because priorities are in the school's annual School Improvement Plan, this serves as a discussion guide in grade level meetings and at the "congress meeting" (where it is formally approved by the staff), and there is "buy-in" by all members of the staff. As a result, there is a strong desire to implement decisions, and the staff does not view lack of funds or support from a level beyond the school as a hindrance to professional development.

Road Bumps

Over the past six years, the school's staff has struggled with many issues while working to refine the governance structure. These "road bumps" have fallen into the areas of effective teaming (collaboratively working together), clear and thorough communication, and the impact of new instructional leaders (especially the position of the principal).

Effective Teaming

Jarboe reports that almost from the beginning, every staff member was surprised by the amount of time it took to work collaboratively in groups to develop consensus. Staff members have little time after school in which to work as a group because of the number of teachers involved in co-curricular activities; over half of the staff works with students after school in sports, clubs, tutorial programs, or the after-school program. Almost all staff members have received staff development on conducting efficient meetings. For example, to remain focused on selected topics, all meetings begin with an agenda and a set time frame for each topic.

Training included a summer retreat, and the staff made the decision to invite all staff members in leadership positions to attend. Participants included Action Team Chairpersons, Grade Level Chairpersons, members of the Steering Committee, Congress meeting co-facilitators, and all administrators. A result of this retreat was the delineation of the roles and responsibilities of the various teams in the school.

The strong emphasis on working collaboratively also proved to be a challenge to staff. When opinions were sought, differing opinions needed to be resolved; however, the resolution of these differing opinions created a stronger understanding of, and commitment to, implementing the decisions of the staff.

Clear and Thorough Communication

As the expectations and traditions of implementing shared governance became more ingrained in the school culture, the staff became aware of the importance of clear communication among all teams regarding decisions made during Congress Meetings and procedures developed to make the governance process more efficient. Accurate record keeping became essential.

During spring 1999, the staff made a decision about what time of the day is best for each grade level (grades 6–8) to have exploratory classes. The following year, no written account of the decision could be located in the minutes of the Congress meetings, and there were varying recollections of what was decided. The importance of accurate record keeping became apparent, and the staff created the position of school historian, whose responsibility is to maintain records of the minutes of all Action Team, Steering Committee, and Congress meetings.

New staff members began to voice concerns that it took over half of the year to understand the process of shared governance. An ad hoc committee formed and met with new staff members to understand their frustrations. Now, at the beginning of each school year, new staff members receive an orientation to shared governance at Coile. The orientation includes the "story" of Coile Middle School, an overview of shared governance, and a review of the Handbook of

Shared Governance, created by teachers. This resource contains the history, procedures, major decisions, and any forms developed by the staff. The handbook is updated each summer, and every staff member receives an updated copy of the handbook annually.

The Impact of New Instructional Leaders

In the past seven years, Coile Middle School has had three different principals, three different assistant principals, and three different instructional lead teachers. The degree to which the principal of a school supports such governance structures is critical to the success of such innovations.

The Clarke County School District uses school-based interview teams for the hiring of new principals. During the hiring of Coile's third principal, the interview team determined that the interview process would center on Coile's shared governance process, and the team would ask for a commitment from the applicant to support it.

Continual Evaluation

The staff and instructional leaders are committed to empowering other teachers through the process of shared governance, and Jarboe emphasizes that his teachers continually wrestle with complex issues concerning the refinement of the process. The staff and the school's Steering Committee wanted to develop a clearer description of how this body decides which issues are part of the shared-governance process and which issues are for the administrative team to handle. The Steering Committee began to research this topic and found that there is little data on such a "nuts-and-bolts" topic. The committee developed an original flow chart detailing how this body makes decisions. As needs arise, the process of shared governance is reevaluated.

The staff of Coile Middle School remains convinced that teacher empowerment does contribute to improved student achievement. During the past two years, the school district's middle schools began using new geographic attendance zones to determine the student populations of the district's middle schools. The poverty rate (measured by free/reduced lunches) at Coile Middle School is now the highest in the district, having increased almost 20 percent.

In 2000–2001, the state of Georgia began administering the Georgia Criterion Reference Competency Test to all 6th- and 8th-grade students. At Coile, the percent of students at the school who met or exceeded state expectations for the mathematics and reading portion of the tests exceeded the district's average in all subgroups (the results are reported according to race, gender, and exceptionality). The staff is convinced that teacher empowerment is essential for the school staff's professional growth, as well as for student growth and achievement.

Duties and Responsibilities of the Instructional Lead Teacher

Development of Site Goals

One of the responsibilities of the ILT is to assist in developing team, grade-level, and school-wide site goals. These goals become the impetus for much of the planning and activities that occurs in the school. The ILT must be familiar with the purpose and function of site goals to aid in their development. Frequently, site goals relate to district-level goals developed at the central-office level, and the ILT needs to align site and district-wide goals. Figure 4.5 offers examples of site-level goals.

Figure 4.5. Site-Level Goals

School-Wide Goal: School Climate

Goal: To maintain student and faculty recognition programs, which result in a positive response from at least 80 percent of respondents on the end of year climate committee survey.

Assessment: Progress on this goal will be monitored through reports and documents offered at monthly committee meetings and by the end-of-year survey results.

Action Plan: Maintain the following programs:

- School awards (discretion of teachers)
- Student of the week and/or month awards
- Faculty Birthdays
- Honor Roll Breakfast
- Newsletter and Web-page recognition
- Awards Assembly

Grade Level Site Goal: Civility

Goal: To promote civility as a tool for lifelong use as indicated by a 10 percent reduction in behavioral referrals and detention assignments.

Assessment: Progress to be monitored in team meetings by viewing disciplinary reports and an end-of-year comparison with the previous year's results.

Action Plan: Themes in advisory activities will focus on civility toward others and being part of a community. Core teachers will emphasize, when possible, civility through learning activities.

Department-Level Site Goal: Curriculum

Goal: To implement strategies that will increase the number of students to at least 70 percent scoring satisfactorily on the geography state-level test while maintaining or increasing scores in other areas.

Assessment: Progress is to be monitored through study of progress reports and related assignments in social studies. Test data from the state will determine the percentage of satisfactory students.

Action Plan: Each teacher in the department will help develop a "practice test" for geography, and will present a geography term of the week.

Used with permission of the Norman Public Schools, Norman, Oklahoma.

Once goals have been developed, it is the duty of the ILT to (a) support the implementation of goals, (b) monitor the achievement of goals, (c) report the progress of goals, and (d) revisit and perhaps revise goals based on lessons learned during the process of goal development and implementation results.

ILTs support the implementation of goals through the decisions that they make. At the forefront of every decision, the ILT needs to ask: *"How will this decision affect the attainment of goals?"* The answer to this question should serve as a guide in making decisions regarding resource allocation—expenditure of funds, energy, and time. The efforts of the ILT need to center on providing the resources for teachers to achieve goals.

The ILT uses a variety of data sources to assess progress toward goals, and Figure 4.6 can assist the ILT to track data.

Figure 4.6. Data Collection and Analysis Matrix

Activities	*Artifacts*	*Analysis of Results*
ILT to computerize discipline contacts and run analysis monthly and then by quarter and semester.	Computer printout of data	Sixth grade students had the greatest number of referrals (tardies during 4th hour—the period after lunch); Team 6, Eagles—6 referrals for going to their lockers between 2nd and 3rd period; Team 6, Hawks—98 referrals for books not being covered.
ILT to share results with administrative team, grade level leaders.	Summary report of data analysis.	
ILT to compile interventions used by team and grade level, and conduct a meeting to discuss effectiveness and modifications.	Meeting agenda. Summary of modifications used by teams.	
ILT will work with teachers in developing an advisory curriculum covering the theme of civility.	The curriculum: lesson plans, instructional materials.	
The ILT will provide coaching to teachers as they implement the civility curriculum.	Coaching log.	
ILT to coordinate efforts of guidance counselor, social worker, and district behavior specialist.	Plans and strategies developed by guidance counselor, social worker.	

Periodically, the ILT will need to report school-wide results of goals, and the results of efforts need to be communicated in a way that others can do something with the results. Parents can be informed of results through many media: the school home page, parent bulletins and newsletters, and presentations made at open houses and parent organization meetings. Professional development should be designed to support progress toward reaching the school's goals.

The Content of Middle School Professional Development

Professional development at the middle school can focus on aspects of teaming, advisory issues, or even the study of the middle school student. As an alternative to school-wide professional development, the faculty may desire or need to participate in activities that provide experiences related to needs across a grade level, by grade level teams, an exploratory team, or by content and subject areas. This type of multifaceted professional development will take extra time and effort to organize, but can address specific needs of the faculty that are unique to middle schools.

Demonstration Lessons

Another way in which the ILT can help to support teacher growth is by providing demonstration lessons. Getting into the classroom provides the ILT with the opportunity to share expertise in the planning and delivery of content and to develop a sense of community with teachers, and is a way to implement peer coaching (pre-observation conference, an extended classroom observation, and a post-observation conference), and to get teachers talking with one another. As a result, the isolation experienced by many teachers may lessen.

Working with Team Leaders: Promoting the Conditions that Foster Interdisciplinary Cooperation

The ILT can provide leadership that assists team leaders and team members to work together across disciplines. Interdisciplinary cooperation is a necessity for the success of the middle school philosophy. If possible, teams should include both veteran teachers and novice teachers. This array of experience and differing views of the profession can serve to get teachers talking about teaching. To keep the talk about teaching moving forward, the ILT needs to facilitate group discussions among teams, by:

- Creating an atmosphere for constructive feedback on suggestions.
- Being open about conflicting ideas and beliefs.
- Maintaining a goal-oriented environment.

♦ Continuing communication with other team members between meetings.

Guidance in the area of team planning is also an important role for ILTs. The common plan time for middle school teams is central to the success of the middle school philosophy; wise use of time is important. The need for an instructional unit may originate from a site goal, a perceived student need, or a district or state standard. The benefits of the unit should be made clear to both teachers and students. Finally, some form of timely assessment of the unit and its implementation needs to be a priority to promote reflection on results and possible modification of goals.

McQuaide (1994) offers the following suggestions that the ILT may pass along to Team Leaders for alternative use of team planning time:

♦ Developing a self-evaluation mechanism for curricular units and for the effectiveness of the team meetings themselves.

♦ Receiving guidance from a district expert or the development of new goals.

♦ Becoming a study group for exploring professional literature.

♦ Facilitating individual and group reflection.

♦ Planning and conducting peer coaching and other professional-development activities.

The Middle School Team Leader

The leadership of the team leader can be summed up in one word—*connections*. The role of the team leader is to connect the teachers on the team, the students with the planned curriculum, the team members to other teams, and the team itself to other teams, as well as to administrators, counselors, and the community the school serves. This connective function is highly important to the educational organization, and is critical to the development of the faculty and students within the middle school. The team leader must be a facilitator, a negotiator, an innovator, and a motivator.

The leadership role of the team leader is similar to that of a point guard on a basketball team. Although the point guard may use strategies and plays designed by coaches before a game, it is the role of the point guard to lead the team in the execution of those plays while in the game. The point guard is also responsible for getting the ball into the hands of the players who need it, when they need it, and assisting them to evaluate the results. The point guard can control the tempo of a game by changing the structure or strategy employed by the team depending on the situation that is being faced. Just as the point guard's preparation for, and study of, basketball builds trust between team members, so it can be with team leaders. As with the point guard, team leaders take the lead in studying, teaching, and learning, while simultaneously being a member of the team.

What Do Team Leaders Do in the Middle School?

Team leaders not only assist their teams, but they also serve as leaders at the site level as well. Some of the activities that these leaders engage in include:

- Encouraging curriculum innovation and goal-oriented experimentation.
- Preparing and participating in staff-development opportunities.
- Engaging in informal discussions with team members between formal meetings.
- Maintaining a clear understanding of the vision of the district and the site goals, and relating these to team members.
- Making the classroom a model for teaching and learning and encouraging classroom observation by other team members.
- Supporting the team by obtaining and distributing resources equitably among team members.

Team Meetings

Setting the agenda for a team meeting helps to keep meetings on track and productive. A team meeting agenda may be as simple as the one presented in Figure 4.7.

Figure 4.7. Sample Team Meeting Agenda

Agenda for October 16, 2002

- Special Education Concerns:
- Gifted Activities:
- Kid Concerns:
- Counseling Needs:
- Exploratory Team Connections:
- Calendar Review:
- Activities and Events:
- Advisory Issues:
- Duties and Housekeeping:
- Other:

Much of the work accomplished during team meetings centers on student issues through developing strategies for meeting the needs of diverse students—special, gifted, or at-risk. This may require the team leader to schedule a meeting with the principal, a counselor, a gifted coordinator, or the ILT to address these needs before the regularly scheduled team meeting.

Curriculum planning, such as a cross-disciplinary approach (e.g., teaching the metric system within the same time frame throughout all math and science classes), may necessitate a meeting with only science and math team members who teach in these content areas across all grade level teams. There may be specific exploratory team concerns to settle before meeting with an academic team, thus initiating a different meeting structure. The responsibility for determining the meeting schedule and agenda rests squarely on the shoulders of the team leader.

Coupled with curriculum development, the collaboration of the team on individual student concerns and remedies is the most important aspect of the team concept in the middle school. For example, the team leader might track disciplinary problems with the assistant principal and bring the results to the attention of the team. Not all progress reports have to be negative.

Positive recognition forms (see Figure 4.8) serve to focus the team members on what is important in their classrooms—the success of children. Recognizing the individual efforts of students and communicating these to parents will help foster better communication between the team and parents of students. All too often, teachers only contact parents when there is a problem or when a student is already failing a course. Parents need to hear good news about their child, too.

Figure 4.8. Positive Student Recognition Form

We Are Glad You Are a Mercury Middle School Star

_____

(Student Name)

has done something wonderful and we want you to know!

_____
_____
_____
_____
_____

We value the attitude and the accomplishment, and look forward to many more successes in the future!!!!

Sincerely Yours, _____

Apples, Oranges, and Interdisciplinary Team Planning

Interdisciplinary team planning is one of the hallmarks of the middle school concept. The idea that several teachers representing several subjects could plan lessons that overlap, dovetail, or jigsaw may be new to some team members. With newcomers to the profession or to the middle school concept, the team leader orients, inducts, and mentors teachers through the process of interdisciplinary teaming. Trying to synchronize curriculum from language arts, social studies, mathematics, science, fine arts, athletics and life skills classes is like comparing apples and oranges.

Team leaders need to present and model interdisciplinary planning and demonstrate the validity of the student learning that occurs as a result of the teachers' cooperative efforts. Connecting a variety of subjects is much like comparing the proverbial apple and orange. Although apples and oranges are different, they also have similarities—both have skins, have seeds, produce juice, provide flavoring, are fruits, grow on trees, and are used as a food source. Finding overlapping junctures between different content areas provides a starting point for interdisciplinary planning.

During before-school team meetings, team leaders can help teachers identify possible interdisciplinary teaching opportunities by having teachers construct "Big Picture" poster-board-sized charts that have on them all the topics to be learned throughout the year. The team then looks for commonalities, overlaps, and tie-ins within all, or part, of the subject areas (concepts, too) where content overlaps. Some concepts may be *omnidisciplinary* (reaching across all subjects), others may be *multidisciplinary* (encompassing more than two subjects) and still others may be *crossdisciplinary* (two subject areas that overlap). Thematic teaching, in whatever form it takes, should involve:

- Exploration
- Integrated curriculum design
- "Hands-on" instructional practices whenever possible.

The work of the team leader is to facilitate and support the process of bringing to usable form the ideas and plans for thematic teaching units. The team leader needs to be someone who facilitates cooperation and collaboration that, in turn, leads the team to consensus. Polite (1994) outlines the consensus approach to planning:

- Develop a culture of open discussion.
- Each team member is allowed to "have their say" without interruption.
- The team leader and members must be good listeners.
- Multiple teaching experience levels are recognized and celebrated.
- Goal-oriented risk taking is encouraged.
- The culture of the school must also support open consensus-building activities.

Duties and Issues for the Team Leader

Many of the leadership tasks undertaken by team leaders are clearly outlined—almost "official" in nature—but some responsibilities are "unofficial." Whether the duties and issues (set forth below) are formal or informal, the impact on the efficient functioning of the team and the school can be significant.

Hiring New Staff Members

Often, team leaders serve on committees to hire new staff. This assignment, although sometimes time-consuming, is an important one. It is important to understand federal and state statutes and district hiring policies before participating in the process of hiring teachers. What the team leader can bring to the hiring process is a clear picture of what kind of teacher would be the "best fit" with the school philosophy. Some aspects to consider when hiring new staff could include whether the candidate has:

- An understanding of the "middle grade" student academically, physically, socially, and emotionally.
- A positive attitude toward interdisciplinary planning and teaching.
- A willingness to work with other teachers, counselors, gifted coordinators, special education teachers, parents, and outside stakeholders.
- An orientation toward professional growth and development.

The Transition to and from the Middle School

Because they are in the middle of the educational system, middle schools have double duty when it comes to transitioning to and from the site. Teacher leaders work with other stakeholders to effect a smooth transition for incoming sixth graders and outgoing eighth graders. It is critical to develop positive relationships between faculty and support personnel at the elementary and high school levels. A team leader is in a solid position to:

- Communicate with fifth grade administrators, teachers, and counselors.
- Conduct fifth grade "walk-throughs" (train sixth grade student guides).
- Hold after-school hours fifth grade parent/student orientation meetings.
- Orient parents to middle school philosophy and expectations.
- Introduce parents to administrators, counselors and exploratory teachers.
- Explain the advisory and exploratory programs to parents and students.
- Answer academic and school-life questions.

A Case Study from the Field: Camp Turning Points at Whittier Middle School, Norman, Oklahoma

> *Camp Turning Points*
>
> Whittier Middle School
> Mr. Billy Nettles, Principal
> 2000 West Brooks, Norman, OK 73069
> 405-366-5956
> Fax: 405-447-6562
> E-mail: bnettles@norman.k12.ok.us
> Online: www.norman.k12.ok.us
> Norman Public Schools
> Dr. Joseph Siano, Superintendent

Camp Turning Points

Camp Turning Points, a joint endeavor of the Norman, Oklahoma Public Schools and the Oklahoma National Guard demonstrates how elementary and middle school teacher leaders, administrators at each level, and the broader community can work to support students transitioning from the elementary school to the middle school.

History

In 1994, the Oklahoma National Guard and the Norman Public Schools began a partnership to support students' transitions from elementary to middle school. Lynn Miller, then Whittier Middle School Principal, along with Colonel Danny Marler of the Oklahoma National Guard and a group of teacher leaders, developed a daylong "mini-camp" to introduce incoming students to the middle school.

The idea behind Camp Turning Points is to bring together all incoming sixth graders for a smoother transition into middle school. To accomplish this goal, Camp Turning Points groups sixth graders into squads that participate in "bonding activities." These activities create an atmosphere where the sixth graders get to know each other, introduce them to the middle school faculty and staff, and give them the opportunity to get to know the physical layout of their new school. Figure 4.9 offers a sample schedule of activities for Camp Turning Points.

Figure 4.9. Camp Turning Points Schedule of Activities

Time	Event
7:30 to 8:30	Meet with National Guard (coffee and donuts)
8:30 to 9:00	Registration in cafeteria (Teacher Leaders)
9:00 to 9:15	Welcome; Rules for the Day (Principal)
9:15 to 10:20	Team Building—Each platoon is assigned an area and each squad is assigned space within that area. Each squad works together on team-building activities: introductions, birthday line-up, the human knot (squad), brainstorming and designing the squad's banner, human knot (platoon).
9:30 to 10:00	Coordinator meets with parent volunteers
10:30 to 11:30	First two activity rotations
11:30 to 12:00	Lunch
12:00 to 1:30	Finish rotations
1:30 to 2:15	Decorate banners
2:15 to 2:45	Pass and Review (closing ceremony)
2:45 to 3:00	Ice Cream Social

Although its beginnings are at Whittier, the Camp Turning Points program now involves all middle schools in the Norman Public Schools. Each middle school has placed its own stamp on Camp Turning Points. For example, Longfellow Middle School, where Lynn Miller is now principal, has an "Open House" for sixth graders and their parents at the end of the afternoon in place of the group "Pass and Review" activity at other middle schools.

The People

Although Camp Turning Points is supported by administrators from the various middle schools and from personnel from the Oklahoma National Guard, leadership for Camp Turning Points comes from teachers.

The Coordinator

Each principal selects a sixth grade teacher who will serve in two positions: Grade level Coordinator and Camp Turning Points Coordinator. Principals select these teacher leaders based on their demonstrated leadership as teachers, potential for leadership, respect of faculty, staff, administrators, parents, and students.

The Sixth Grade Level Coordinator serves on the Principal's Communication Council (which meets weekly) and that teacher reports back to all other sixth grade team leaders to share information about activities for the school. This person is also responsible for all other activities undertaken yearly by this grade level (e.g., a sixth grade field trip to a museum or the state capitol). The Grade Level Coordinator for sixth grade is also the Coordinator for Camp Turning Points.

Billy Nettles, Principal of Whittier Middle School, reports that although teacher leadership is reviewed on a yearly basis, most teachers serve in a leadership capacity for two or three years before passing the torch to another teacher.

Team Leaders

Sixth grade Team Leaders take charge of various activities and tasks, and they assume some type of leadership role every year; however, all sixth grade teachers are involved in planning, preparing, and supervising some aspect of Camp Turning Points.

National Guardsmen

These volunteers from the local Guard are responsible for leading a squad of students through the day. They also come early (the day before) to set up the "obstacle course" that each squad must traverse together. They concentrate on building teamwork and camaraderie.

Parent Volunteers

Depending on the number of teachers involved, parents can and do help with many of the tasks and events during the day. These activities include handing out shirts, preparing lunch, helping with the scavenger hunt, distributing name tags, and managing supplies for various games.

Action

The Camp Turning Points Coordinator organizes planning sessions with the principal and coordinates with the National Guard representatives who also attend planning sessions. The Coordinator assigns areas (e.g., scavenger hunt) to team leaders for their supervision. The coordinator also is responsible for working with the fifth grade teachers, principals, counselors, and parents as needed. A sixth grade teacher is in charge of the skit that students write and produce and that former sixth grade students perform.

The final activity of the camp is a "Pass and Review" by each squad with their Guard leader displaying the squad banner that they made during the day. At this time, the coordinator, team leaders, sixth grade teachers, and middle school administrators are introduced to all of the new students and their parents.

Evaluation

After the event, the Principal, Coordinator, and Team Leaders meet to discuss the entire event to determine what was successful, what was not, and new ideas or twists that might make a better transitioning activity. The Coordinator then makes revisions in the current Camp Turning Points manual.

Transitioning from Middle School to High School

To facilitate the transition from middle school to high school, the team leader can:

- Coordinate all activities with high school counselors and, when possible, ninth grade teachers.
- Facilitate student record transfers, particularly those of middle school students who have completed courses for high school credit while at the middle school.
- Attend and encourage attendance of students and parents at high school–sponsored night meeting.
- Accompany the eighth graders on tours of the high school.
- Address academic concerns of students and parents.
- Introduce graduation requirements.
- Give as many descriptions of elective classes as possible.
- Outline types and uses of testing.
- Introduce the concept of college, vo-tech or other post–high school options available.
- Help assist the high school counselors with student scheduling.

Balancing the Core and Exploratory Programs

One of the easiest avenues to team discontent is through the perception that one element of the team is not as valued as another one. In some instances, schools and school leaders place a strong emphasis on the core subjects (math, science, English) because these are the subjects that are most often tested and that are understood by the public to be important in developing an economically fit society. Even in schools that maintain a culture of equality, exploratory teachers can sometimes feel marginalized. The team leader needs to place extra emphasis on team building in the exploratory areas. An understanding of the "performance centered" nature of many exploratory programs is essential to creating a valid, trusting relationship between the team leader and the exploratory teachers.

Although each subject is different, the exploratory curriculum needs the same rigor as the core curriculum, and expectations should be just as high for student achievement. The team leader needs to take every opportunity to include exploratory subjects in each "theme" of the integrated curriculum. One of the tenets of middle school philosophy is exploration by the students. The team leader can establish and maintain an atmosphere where exploratory programs and teachers are held in high esteem, and where they are valued members of the team.

Award Ceremonies and Guest Speakers

Team leaders often coordinate student award ceremonies, and they find ways to recognize the accomplishments of teachers as well. Student and faculty recognition are esteem builders and serve to motivate. The payoff is usually positive for the individual honored, for those in attendance, and for boosting school climate.

Guest speakers can have a positive impact in the middle school setting. At an age when students are growing, questioning, and challenging, outside experts can aid in the educational process. As a team leader, it is beneficial to develop relationships through the community and nearby colleges or universities. Team leaders can encourage team members to help to find reputable and relevant speakers who can relate to the middle school student. Very often, it falls to the team leader to coordinate schedules, secure funding, and to seek approval for a guest speaker.

Chapter Summary

Instructional Lead Teachers and Team Leaders, for the most part, practice connective leadership. Through respectful, open, and goal-centered team meetings, the teams connect to one another. The interdisciplinary approach to curriculum development connects subject to subject. Students connect to life through the curriculum and activities, and they are nurtured by a safe and open school climate. The team leader connects the team to the school and the district through support services, information exchanges, resource allocation, and representation on committees. The team leader also plans and organizes the connection of the middle school to the elementary and high school levels. By being a facilitator, mediator and innovator, the team leader and the Instructional Lead Teacher can ensure an effective and invigorating team environment that will benefit and connect the students, the school, the district, and the community.

References

McQuaide, J. (1994). Implementation of team planning time. *Research in Middle Level Education*, 17(2), 27–45.

Polite, M. M. (1994). Team negotiation and decision-making: Linking leadership to curricular and instructional innovation. *Research in Middle Level Education*, 18(1), 65–81.

5
Teacher Leadership in the High School

In this Chapter

- Perspectives about leadership at the high school level
- The high school department chair
- Getting started
- The work of department chairs
  - The beginning and ending of the school year
  - Managing the department budget
  - Managing facilities and equipment
  - Conducting department meetings
  - Serving as a content specialist
  - Developing curriculum guides
  - Handling student placement issues
  - Interviewing teacher candidates for the department
  - Building accountability: Profiling the department's accomplishments
  - Writing reports and forecasting needs
- Balancing departmental work with the duties of a teacher

Introducing Teacher Leadership in the High School

American high schools offer a more diverse and complex curriculum than ever before. Advances in technology, the evolving needs of an increasingly diverse society, and intensified standards of accountability through statutory mandates make it necessary for principals to seek additional sources of leadership. Perhaps the most common source of leadership in high schools is the department chair. However, there are many other formal and informal opportunities for teacher leaders. Much of the focus of this chapter is primarily on the work that department chairs do; however, other teacher leaders, such as grade-level coordinators and committee chairs can find the discussion of the work of teacher leadership and the department chair equally beneficial.

Perspectives about Teacher Leadership at the High School Level

The most stable unit of any high school is the department, comprised of teachers, and in most departments there is an appointed or elected leader—the department chair. In some states, the department chair is an administrator by virtue of certification and has the ability to legally evaluate teachers. However, not every state or school system requires the department chair to be a certified administrator. For the most part, the division of the high school by departments represents four key aspects of how schools work in those departments:

1. Represent a strong boundary in dividing the school
2. Provide a primary site for social interaction
3. Have, as administrative units, considerable discretion over the micro-political decisions affecting what and how teachers teach
4. Influence the decisions and shape the actions of those who inhabit them. (Siskin, 1991, p. 34)

In large, super-size high schools, the department chair might be the only leader with whom teachers come in contact, and the department chair is responsible for focusing the efforts of the unit, representing the needs of the unit to the administrative team, and lobbying for finite resources. Within the structure of the department, there are numerous opportunities for others to work as leaders.

Teachers assume leadership when they serve on accreditation teams, represent their grade level at school-wide and district committees, and coordinate subject-matter articulation between and among grade levels. Moreover, given the structure of the high school, teacher leaders serve on school-wide committees such as the School Improvement Council, Principal Advisory Committee, or as school-wide representative to civic organizations, community partnership initiatives, and district-wide committees.

The High School Department Chair

The high school department chair is, perhaps, the most visible teacher leader. High school department chairs serve as instructional leaders, inventory and budget managers, public relations officers, and, in most cases, another

Teacher Leadership in the High School

teacher on the faculty. This chapter offers a description of the work of high school department chairs and provides some commonly needed tools that can help support all facets of the department chair's work as leader.

Although much of this chapter focuses on the work of the high school department chair, teacher leaders at this level, regardless of title, formality of leadership, or experience with leadership, should read on with the knowledge that the skills in this chapter cut across leadership. For example, grade level leaders and school improvement committee chairs develop agendas, work with colleagues to align curriculum, and serve on interview teams. Regardless of the work, teacher leaders step up to the plate and make positive contributions to the overall effectiveness of the school, and this is the focus of this chapter.

Getting Started

As is the case for beginning teachers, administrators, and others new to a position, the first days on the job as a high school department chair produce a combination of excitement and apprehension. New department chairs are excited about the new challenges and responsibilities and, at the same time, are somewhat apprehensive about them. Although the work and the roles of the department chair tend to be context-specific, some commonalities exist with the work and roles of other positions at the school. The work of department chairs cast them into roles—instructional leader, curriculum coordinator, business manager, and public relations officer. However, department chairs often serve as teacher confidants, student advocates, and mediators. Learning how to be an effective high school department chair begins with the identification of the specific expectations of site and district administrators. The following four strategies can help new high school department chairs to identify the work, expectations, and roles they will assume:

1. Secure a copy of the job description.
2. Review the site faculty handbook.
3. Schedule a meeting with the administration.
4. Find a mentor.

Secure a Copy of the Job Description

Most school districts have written job descriptions for high school department chairs, and it is important for the new chair to locate a copy of the district-approved job description. The job description (Figure 5.1) offers important insights into administrative expectations for department chairs.

Figure 5.1. High School Department Chair Job Description

Anytown Public School District
Job Description: High School Department Chair

Qualifications: A master's degree with emphasis in the content area, three years of teaching experience (at least one must be in the Anytown District), and the ability to work with colleagues, administrators, parents, and the public.

Reports to: Principal/Assistant Principal for Curriculum and Instruction

Responsibilities:

- Models exemplary teaching techniques specific to the content area.
- Conducts monthly department meetings.
- Conducts regular observations of department members' teaching, acts as a coach for department members, and makes recommendations to the principal regarding departmental personnel.
- Provides for the induction and mentoring of new department members.
- Provides regular in-service opportunities for the department members.
- Manages department inventory (furniture, instructional supplies, office equipment, other materials specific to the department's discipline) including purchasing/ordering.
- Assists the principal in articulating the department's programs and needs to the Board of Education, parents, and other stakeholders.
- Assists the principal in the interviewing and hiring of new staff members for the department.
- Develops and maintains a library of professional materials relevant to the department's curriculum and programs.
- Develops and supports a continuous plan for developing and evaluating the department's curriculum, including preparing curriculum guides, building a library of sample lesson plans, participating in textbook adoption, and conducting the department's comprehensive program evaluation plan.
- Other duties as assigned by the principal.

Anytown School District is an Equal Opportunity Employer

Careful analysis of the job description's content provides insight about job expectations for the new department chair. In addition to the district-approved job description, the site faculty handbook is also useful.

Review the Site Faculty Handbook

Although the district job description normally provides the "broad strokes" of the job, the site faculty handbook provides specifics about the day-to-day operations of the school and, by extension, the work of department chairs within the school. Examination of this document will yield important insights into the specific expectations of site administrators. Some questions for the department chair to ask include:

- Which tasks (or types of tasks) are specifically reserved for the department chairs?
- Which tasks are emphasized (printed in bold, italics, or underlined; referenced multiple times)?
- For what kind of assistance will faculty most often consult the department chair?

After examining the site faculty handbook, the new department chair can compare its contents to that of the job description and ask:

- Do these documents emphasize the same tasks?
- Do the documents seem to portray the same expectations for the job?

It is important to realize that how the job is conceptualized in the district-approved job description and how the job plays out at the site are not necessarily the same. One strategy to help reconcile any conflicts between these two documents is to engage the site administration in a discussion about the work of the position.

Schedule a Meeting with the Administration

Whereas some high school administrative teams are limited to the principal only, others include assistant principals, associate principals, and, perhaps, administrative assistants. Regardless of the administrative configuration, there will always be an administrator assigned to work with each department chair. A discussion between the department chair and the administrator is an important step for new department chairs seeking to understand their new work and role within the structure of the school.

As important as understanding the expectations of the department chair's work from the job description and the site faculty handbook is gaining an understanding of how the assigned administrator interprets those expectations. Areas to explore during this meeting should address the assigned administrator's expectations for the department chair in the areas of instructional leadership, facilities management, and program evaluation. Figure 5.2 can assist new department chairs to frame the expectations of their work and role.

Figure 5.2. Framing the Expectations of the Work as Department Chair

Area	Expectations
Instructional Leadership	Informal and formal supervision, textbook adoption, development of curriculum guides, mentoring new teachers.
Facilities Management	Assignment of classroom space including auxiliary spaces used beyond traditional instruction (e.g., the gym, the stage and auditorium, playing fields).
Program Evaluation	Impact on instruction across grade levels, subject areas; analysis of test data (e.g., ACT, SAT); failure rates across grade and subject areas; dropout rates.

Schools are complex organizations and so, too, the work of department chairs and other teacher leaders is equally complex. Teacher leaders not only need to understand their work, but they also need to understand the complexities of interacting with coworkers in ways that are different from when they were teachers. Motivating adults is more complex than motivating students, communicating with adults is different than with students, and learning how to develop as a leader within the broader context of the school and department is equally difficult as, but different from, emerging as a leader with students in the confines of a single classroom. Finding a mentor can ease the transition from teacher leader in the classroom to leader of leaders with teachers.

Find a Mentor

Just as a new teacher needs a mentor, so does a new department chair. A mentor who is already serving as a department chair can assist the novice to "learn the ropes." This mentor is in a unique position to support the new chair in learning how to complete and submit paperwork, or how to help teachers who are experiencing difficulties in the classroom. New department chairs can ask the administrator who oversees the department to suggest another department chair to serve in this vital role.

Often, the former department chair will still be a member of the department, and there is an upside and a downside to asking the former department chair to mentor a new chair. Whether the former department chair mentors the new chair will depend on the context of the setting: namely, whether the former chair left the position on good terms or not. It would be disastrous for the former chair to mentor a new chair if the predecessor left the position on a "sour" note. In addition, as a new chair, it is advisable to remain free of "political entanglements" and to emerge as a leader who is not part of the "old guard."

The Work of Department Chairs

Department chairs, regardless of the amount of time released from teaching, assume responsibility for not only the curriculum, but also for the people in the department—teachers and the students they teach. Moreover, department chairs assume responsibility for:

- Coordinating activities for the beginning and ending of the school year
- Managing the department budget
- Ensuring that facilities and equipment are ready for student and faculty use
- Conducting department meetings
- Serving as a content specialist
- Developing curriculum guides
- Handling student placement issues
- Interviewing teacher candidates for the department
- Building accountability by profiling the department's accomplishments
- Writing reports and forecasting needs

Familiarity with these areas will enhance the work of the department chair, and although some of the work associated with these areas is managerial, mastery and proficiency will help the department chair to emerge as a credible leader capable of "clearing the way" for teachers in their departments to be leaders—both in and out of the classroom.

Coordinating Activities for the Beginning and Ending of the School Year

Teachers and administrators alike find the beginning and the ending of a school year hectic. As a new school year begins, teachers are preparing instruction, setting up classrooms, and attending meetings. Administrators plan meetings, enroll students, and check inventories. At the end of the school year, teachers are writing and grading final exams, inventorying classroom equipment and furnishings, and calculating grades. Administrators are collecting teachers' paperwork, preparing next year's teaching schedule, and writing end-of-the-year reports for the district and the state. In the case of high school department chairs, the beginning and ending of a school year present unique challenges—they do *both* sets of tasks. Department chairs who work in schools using block scheduling will be required to complete beginning- and end-of-year tasks more than once each year—at the beginning and ending of each semester.

The novice department chair can feel overwhelmed at the beginning and ending of a school year. Familiarity with the forms used at the school site and awareness of deadlines will assist the department to organize time more efficiently. Gaining familiarity with the myriad forms a school uses can be a daunting task, but one that is manageable through organization and advanced planning. The following figure can assist the new department chair in organizing forms by using a three-ring binder separated into sections.

Figure 5.3. Organizing Forms and Deadlines

School-Wide Forms	*Used for Requisitioning*
Maintenance	Repairs for furniture in classroom; maintenance requests
Instructional Materials	Orders for textbooks, supplementary materials
Personnel	Substitutes for teachers who will be out of the building for field trips, staff development
Scheduling	Making changes in student schedules
Budget	Materials both instructional and other

Managing the Department Budget

The array of equipment necessary for the operation of a comprehensive high school is staggering. Math departments use graphics calculators; science labs need test tubes, chemicals, and dissection specimens; social studies teachers use maps and globes; music teachers require sheet music, instruments, and uniforms; and athletic coaches would have a difficult time without sports and safety equipment and uniforms. Because the department chair is a content specialist, most high schools assign the task of choosing the equipment that the department needs to the department chair. Customarily, these materials are purchased through the departmental budget.

Managing the department's budget requires two major skills: *oversight* and *negotiation*. Oversight refers to ensuring that policies are followed and that the department spends within the limits of its budget. All school districts have policies in place to account for the district's money. It is the department chair's responsibility to make sure the required procedures are followed, the proper forms are filled out, and that all necessary paperwork is submitted promptly to the appropriate site administrator and district offices. It is the chair's responsibility to ensure that expenditures stay within the limits prescribed by the administration. A simple budget form, such as the one presented in Figure 5.4, can assist the chair in this process.

Figure 5.4. Department Budget Management Form

Social Studies Department Budget Management Form			
Date, Description, and Vendor	**Purchase Order Number**	**Cost**	**Balance**
Beginning Balance			$500.00
8/31/01 Cases of copy paper County Office Supply Warehouse	200134012	$76.23	$423.77
9/04/01 Set of wall maps for Ms. Smith's room Kramer Map Company	200134014	$82.43	$341.34

Because resources are limited, department chairs need to work with members to decide how to spend money. One approach is to ask members to submit requests. If the total requests exceed available funds, the negotiation process begins. Prioritization of funding requests is essential. Two options can assist department chairs to find additional sources of funds. First, in some situations, two or more departments can pool their resources to cover a large purchase that will satisfy the needs of both departments. A second option is to apply for grants from local, state, or national foundations.

Managing Facilities and Equipment

Department chairs also manage facilities and equipment. From rehearsal halls to science labs, proper scheduling for the use of facilities and equipment allows equal access to department members and, by extension, helps to provide equal educational opportunities for all students. In addition to managing rooms, department chairs manage inventories of musical instruments, calculators, maps, test tubes, sewing machines, and audiovisual equipment. Managing inventories consists of tracking equipment usage; ensuring equipment is in working condition; and replacing consumable materials.

Tracking Usage

By tracking usage, chairs are able to ensure equal access by all department members and to secure equipment when needed. A sample tracking form (Figure 5.5) can be helpful.

Figure 5.5. Equipment Usage Tracking Form

Date Out	Date Back	Description and Condition	Teacher
Aug. 28, 2001	Aug. 29, 2001	TV and VCR with cart and remote Condition: OK	Carter
Aug. 30, 2001	Aug. 31, 2001	TV and VCR with cart and remote Condition: OK	Ferguson

Maintaining the Department's Equipment

Equally as important as tracking usage, equipment must be maintained in good working order. Although the rising cost of repairs has limited equipment repairs or replacement, expensive items such as copying machines, computers, weight machines, and school-owned musical instruments will periodically need maintenance work. A maintenance record for each of these pieces of equipment is suggested. Figure 5.6 serves as an example.

Figure 5.6. Maintenance Repair Record—Copy Machine

Date and Purchase Order Number	Work Done	By Whom	Meter Reading (Number of Copies)
Sept. 1, 2001 200142931	Clean drum, paper feeder	Local Canon Copy Services	8,428

Replacing Consumable Equipment

Some equipment, such as copy machine paper and toner, chemicals and specimens in the science lab, workbooks, calculator batteries, and lubricants for band instruments are consumable. The beginning and ending of the school year are typical times to reorder consumable material because the amount ordered depends on student enrollment.

Serving as a Content Specialist

Patterned after the university system, high schools are organized by content area. As a content specialist, the department chair has three major responsibilities:

1. To be a resource person with content expertise for other department members.
2. To assist the administration in making teaching assignments based on each department member's strengths.
3. To act as a collection point for the combined expertise of all department members.

Although final decisions on teaching assignments normally reside with the principal, and decisions are dependent on certification, the department chair is familiar with the strengths of each department member. Therefore, the department chair's input on teaching assignments is valuable to building the master schedule. Figure 5.7 offers a form to track department members' strengths.

Figure 5.7. Tracking Teacher Content Strengths, Interests, and Instructional Expertise

Teacher	Courses Certified to Teach	Areas of Expertise	Instructional Expertise
Delk	Advanced Placement Biology, Biology I, Biology II, Botany I, Human Anatomy	DNA coding, research on RNA	Cooperative learning
Greenwood	Advanced Placement Chemistry, Chemistry I, Chemistry II, Physics I, Physics II	Law of inertia, balancing chemical equations	Socratic questioning techniques
Temple	Biology I, Chemistry I, Scientific Method	Researching the use of the scientific method in conducting experiments	Simulations

Conducting Department Meetings

Department meetings serve a variety of purposes, and quality department meetings address multiple needs. Among these are to distribute information, to discuss problems of instruction, to make curricular decisions, to allocate materials and resources, and to build collaborative relationships among members of the department. By making the most of department meeting time, chairs let their department members know that their time is respected and valued. Figure 5.8 is a sample department meeting agenda that is useful in this regard.

Figure 5.8. Sample Department Meeting Agenda

March 5, 2002

- Communication/Information/Announcements
    - Parent–Teacher Conferences next Thursday
    - Progress reports due tomorrow
- Instructional Issues
    - Discussion on using cooperative learning
    - Classroom observation schedule
    - Open discussion—current concerns
- Curriculum
    - Discuss scheduling a meeting with representatives from feeder middle schools (vertical teaming)
    - Progress on completing curriculum guides for each course
- Materials, Budget, Inventories
    - Orders for teaching materials are due today
    - Budget requests are due by March 15
- Other

Tips for Running an Effective Department Meeting

Effective department meetings start with a carefully planned agenda, and meetings begin and end on time. Teachers assume a variety of responsibilities (e.g., coaching, moderating student activities, serving on committees outside of the department and school); therefore, sensitivity to other demands on teachers' time is important. To avoid wasting time, agenda items focus on current issues within the department and school, and meetings are limited to relevant discussion.

Preparing the Agenda

An effective meeting begins with a carefully planned agenda. An agenda can provide the chair with a tool for managing the length of the meeting, keeping the discussion on track, and informing the participants on how long of a meeting to expect. Distributing the agenda a few days in advance of the meeting increases the likelihood that department members will come more prepared to take care of business. The agenda also serves as a reminder of the meeting and as a tool to help the chair get organized.

Preparing an agenda is a process, and successful department chairs enlist input from members of the department while developing a meeting agenda. One way to enlist input is to ask for agenda items through a short memo a week or two before the scheduled meeting. Figure 5.9 is a sample memo to solicit input on developing a departmental agenda.

Figure 5.9. Sample Memo Soliciting Agenda Items

Memo

DATE: March 15, 2002
TO: All English Department Members
FROM: Jamie Frost
RE: Agenda Items for the March 29 Meeting

Our monthly meeting is just around the corner, and I am building the meeting agenda. We need to revisit the ACT Preparation Curriculum, an item left over from our last meeting. To help frame our discussion, I have attached some materials gleaned from a conference Margie Reyes attended last week. So far, other items include closure on ordering textbook replacements, and assessing our technology needs for next year. Let me know if there are other items to include on the agenda. I would like to get the agenda finalized within the next week, so please get agenda items to me by March 21.

In advance, thanks for your input.

Because they are a matter of public record, agendas are best kept in an accessible location. An effective way to store agendas is to use a three-ring binder and to then attach the summary or minutes of each meeting after the agenda. At the end of the year, this information can help the chair to review department accomplishments and to develop follow-up plans for the next year.

Beginning and Ending on Time

Teachers, by the nature of their job, are busy people. Understandably, teachers prize their time and do not want it wasted. Beginning and ending the department meeting on time signals to teachers that the chair respects their time and, by extension, respects them as professionals.

Sensitivity in Scheduling Department Meetings

When scheduling department meetings, chairs need to take into consideration the other demands currently being placed on members' time. For example, scheduling a department meeting on the same day as parent–teacher conferences, or on the day progress reports are due, would probably be a poor idea. Unnecessarily overburdening teachers is likely to cause resentment and limit the effectiveness of future department meetings.

Focus on Current Issues within the Department

Although long-term planning is important in any school, current issues should be the focus of department meetings. There are two reasons for this tip. First, the time available for department meetings is usually limited. Second, the more distant a future event is, the more likely the details are to change.

Limit Discussion to the Issues Relevant to the Items on the Agenda

The purpose of preparing an agenda is to decide which items are of sufficient importance to warrant the expenditure of meeting time. Teachers tend to be willing to discuss issues relevant to their classrooms, the department, and the school. No one wants to attend meetings where irrelevant discussion dominates time. Although it is important to allow teachers the opportunity to express their opinions and to generate creative thinking, too much latitude in discussion can have negative results. Department meetings can become mired in nonproductive chat or disintegrate into "gripe" sessions.

Developing Curriculum Guides

Curriculum guides customarily contain a list of topics to be covered, suggestions about the sequence of topics, and expected student outcomes. Although teachers need some flexibility in planning instruction, for every course there are specific objectives that need to be taught. Developing curriculum guides can help ensure that students taking sequential courses (for example, Algebra I and Algebra II) have the prerequisite skills to be successful in the next course, regardless of teacher assignment for the first course. Curriculum guides are also useful in vertical articulation—coordinating the high school curriculum with that of feeder middle schools. For example, by coordinating with the eighth grade music curriculum, high school music teachers have some assurance that entering music students will be ready for the high school curriculum. Curriculum guides can also assist with preparing students for state-mandated achievement tests by cueing teachers to content that needs to be taught and the resources available to them.

Handling Student Placement Issues

Placing students in the proper courses is essential to student success. Students who are not challenged become bored, whereas students "in over their heads," feel overwhelmed. Neither situation is conducive to student learning. Although different content areas present various challenges, three major issues in student placement confront high school department chairs. These issues are (a) sequential courses, (b) honors or advanced placement courses, and (c) programs that include tryouts, such as fine arts and athletics.

Sequential Courses

In many content areas, student success in one course is essential for student success in the next. Examples abound in such areas as mathematics, foreign language, and science. Because of the sequential nature of courses in some content areas, a policy that establishes the level of mastery necessary for a student to progress to the next course may be needed. A proposal to establish such a policy, including the rationale for establishing the policy, should be submitted to the administration for consideration by the board of education or others who would need to defend the outcome if a decision were to be challenged by a student or parent. Such a policy establishes for students a specific criterion required for enrollment in the next course and provides the department chair with evidence to support student placement decisions when questioned by parents.

Honors and Advanced Placement Classes

Nearly all high schools offer honors courses or advanced placement courses. The intent of these courses is to offer an appropriately challenging curriculum for highly talented students. For this reason, high schools traditionally have a required benchmark for students who wish to enroll in these special courses—usually a minimum score on an achievement test. However, should a student who scores one percentile shy of the required benchmark be denied admission to the course? Sometimes, placement decisions relating to such borderline students are contested. For this reason, a process through which placement decisions can be appealed is needed. This process should be approved by the board of education.

Tryouts in the Fine Arts and Athletics

In areas such as the fine arts, students can be required to audition to earn the right to enroll in an advanced course. The department chair needs to ensure that the process is fair to all students, and that the process is in place before tryouts start. The description of the process should include information such as how tryouts will be conducted, who will make the final decisions, what criteria will be used, and how students and parents or guardians will be informed of the results.

Interviewing Teacher Candidates for the Department

In many high schools, the department chair assumes leadership in interviewing prospective teacher candidates. For this reason, it is important for high school department chairs to know how to select candidates, to know what to ask and, perhaps more importantly, what *not* to ask. The hiring process begins with the paper screening. Before screening candidates, the department chair should develop a profile of the type of faculty member being sought. Does this person necessarily need experience? Are there specific courses that the new teacher will teach? Is there specific instructional expertise being sought in the new faculty member? After developing a profile, candidates who most closely resemble that profile are contacted and interviews are scheduled.

Interviewing Teaching Candidates

When preparing to interview candidates for a teaching vacancy, it is important for the department chair to have relevant questions prepared and written down in the order in which they will be asked. Consistency across all interviews enhances fair evaluation of teaching candidates. Job interviews usually involve four objectives:

1. *Evaluation*: collecting knowledge about the candidate to rate his/her suitability and fit for the vacant position.

2. *Information*: providing the applicant with sufficient information so that he/she can make an informed decision about accepting a job offer.

3. *Selling*: influencing a candidate that fits all criteria for the vacant position.

4. *Goodwill*: establishing a positive relationship with each candidate so that goodwill is created and maintained toward the school district. (Stevens, 1981, p. 45)

Effective job interviews consist of different types of questions. Commonly used types of questions include motivation questions, pedagogical questions, character questions, and stress questions. Figure 5.10 provides examples of each type of question.

Figure 5.10. Types of Interview Questions

Type of Question	Example
Motivation Question—designed to explore why a candidate chose a particular profession or applied for a specific position.	Why did you decide to become a teacher?
Pedagogical Question—designed to explore the candidate's knowledge of teaching techniques or the content area.	How would you go about planning a unit on solving quadratic equations?
Character Questions—designed to determine how compatible with the other department members a candidate might be.	How would you work with other department members with an instructional issue?
Stress Questions—designed to determine how a candidate might handle a "real-life" teaching situation.	A student in your classroom refuses to participate in the learning activities you have planned. What would you do?

The types of questions in Figure 5.10 can assist the department chair to gain a comprehensive view of each candidate. However, department chairs need to be aware of questions that legally *cannot* be asked.

Interviewing and the Law

Although it is important for an interviewer to gain as much information as possible about job candidates, some areas are off limits. Two simple rules should help a department chair avoid trouble in the interview:

1. Do not ask about any characteristic of the applicant that the law prohibits you from considering in making your decision (race, religious preference, age, marital status, citizenship, disability); and,

2. Respect the applicant's privacy (Do not ask about an applicant's sex life, for example). (Delpo, 2001, p. 1)

Figure 5.11 provides a list of some of the most important statutes that govern what can and cannot be asked in a job interview.

Figure 5.11. Statutes and Interviewing

Statute	*Areas Addressed*
Title VII of the Civil Rights Act of 1964	Prohibits employers from discriminating against applicants and employees on the basis of race, religion, gender, national origin.
The Age Discrimination in Employment Act of 1967 (29 U.S.C. §§ 621–634)	Prohibits employers from discriminating against persons 40 years of age or older.
The Equal Pay Act of 1963 (29 U.S.C. § 206 (d))	Requires employers to pay men and women equal pay for the same work.
The Immigration Reform and Control Act of 1986 (8 U.S.C. § 1324)	Prohibits employers from discriminating against applicants or employees on the basis of their citizenship or national origin.
The Americans with Disabilities Act of 1990 (42 U.S.C. §§ 12101–12213)	Prohibits employers from discriminating against applicants or employees on the basis of disabilities. Also prohibits employers from discriminating against an applicant or employee on the basis that a relative or associate has a disability.

There is one narrow exception to employment discrimination laws: the bona fide occupational qualification (BFOQ). An applicant can be discriminated against based on gender, religion, national origin, or age *if* the nature of the job requires this type of discrimination. However, race can *never* be a BFOQ. If there is any doubt about a proposed interview question, either the school attorney should be consulted or, perhaps, the question should be dropped.

Writing Reports, Forecasting Needs: Profiling and Publicizing the Department's Accomplishments

Communicating the department's mission and sharing its accomplishments with those stakeholders outside the school is important. Stakeholders include central office administrators, the board of education, parents, and patrons of the school district. The four major purposes of communication include informing, planning, asking, and evaluating.

Communication that Informs

One of the jobs of the department chair is to keep parents and the public informed about the department's accomplishments and activities. The "public relations" work of the department might include press releases for the local print and broadcast media, the school district's print and broadcast media, as well as the school's web site. Press releases should address student and faculty honors and accomplishments, new course offerings, and other noteworthy events. Good public relations can help support the overall efforts of the department to accomplish goals.

Communication that Helps Plan

Preparing reports for the central office or the board of education is a part of the planning process. These reports usually contain a summary of past performance, current programs and course offerings, and a forecast of future needs. The information in these reports can assist in making curricular, personnel, and budgetary decisions. Past meeting agendas and summaries can assist in framing long-term planning and tracking long-term goal attainment.

Communication that Asks

Because school budgets always seem to be tight, department chairs need to "think outside the box" in obtaining needed resources for the department. Many times, local businesses are glad to donate items to support the school's program. For some needs, a personal call to the business will result in meeting a need; however, for more expensive items, the chair may need to apply for a grant. Individual foundations and businesses that fund grants normally provide specific instructions concerning the application process.

In addition to obtaining funds and equipment, department chairs are in a solid position to enlist volunteer support to assist with department events. Building contacts among parents, school patrons, and other stakeholders can assist the department chair in locating the best people for help with special needs and events. The astute department chair checks with the administration to see if there are policies in place to help screen potential volunteers from outside of the school community. In most districts, applicants are screened and background checks are completed to ensure the future safety and well-being of children. The same standard of care needs to be applied to potential volunteers.

Communication that Evaluates

Because of his/her expertise in the content area, the department chair is required to take the lead supplying the information needed to conduct an evaluation of the department's programs and course offerings. The specific information required in this type of report can vary depending on the school and the department. Generally, the information included in evaluation reports consists of courses offered, enrollment trends, grade distributions, relevant college entrance-exam scores, standardized test results, and results of contests in which students have participated. It is important to remember that program evaluation needs to be data driven.

Balancing Departmental Work with the Duties of a Teacher

The work of the high school department chair is largely defined by local needs and customs. In some areas, department chairs are teachers who spend a couple of days per month helping the principal. In others, department chairs are full-time administrators who supervise and evaluate teachers. However, in most cases, department chairs are full- or part-time teachers who also serve as part-time administrators. To be effective in this dual role, high school department chairs must gain entrée into the world of the administrator and, simultaneously, remain accepted in the world of the teachers. For the department chair, operating in the "two worlds" can create tension.

The Administrator–Teacher Tension

Most department chairs spend the majority of their time teaching. They write lesson plans, deliver instruction, and prepare assessments for their students. At the same time, department chairs are administrators. They make budgetary decisions, supervise teachers, and make personnel recommendations to the principal. When a department member consults with the chair, the question is raised: Is this a consultation between equals or is there a hierarchy involved? The uneasy answer is "both." Perhaps a more important question for the novice department chair is how to handle this tension.

Offering a general prescription for handling this tension is slippery because the department chair's situation tends to be locally defined. However, a couple of suggestions are offered. First, chairs need to remember that they began as teachers and still are teachers. Therefore, department members will need to feel safe in asking for advice or help with instructional issues. If the chair is viewed as "having forgotten" from where she has come, then trust between the chair and members of the department can be difficult to build and maintain over time.

Second, novice department chairs need to understand that not every instructional issue in the department merits administrative intervention. Many instructional issues are best solved between colleagues; however, there are exceptions. Discriminating between the two comes with experience.

A Case Study from the Field: TALENT—Teachers as Leaders: Encouraging New Thought—at Shiloh High School, Snellville, Georgia

> *TALENT—Teachers as Leaders: Encouraging New Thought—A Leadership Opportunity for Veteran Teachers*
>
> Shiloh High School, Gwinnett County, GA
> Dr. Jim Kahrs, Principal, Shiloh High School
> Dr. Lea Arnau, Director of Staff Development, Gwinnett County
> 4210 Shiloh Road, Snellville, GA 30039
> (770) 972-8471
> Fax: (770) 736-4345
> E-mail: jkahrs@gwinnett.k12.ga.us
> E-mail: lmarnau@gwinnett.k12.ga.us
> Online: www.shilohhighschool.org
> Mr. J. Alvin Wilbanks, Superintendent

TALENT—Teachers as Leaders: Encouraging New Thought—A Leadership Opportunity for Veteran Teachers

High school department chairs, as well as other teachers in formal and informal leadership positions (grade level leaders, team leaders), sometimes attempt to increase their leadership capacity by enlisting the assistance of other department, team, or grade level members. By increasing the participation of department members in work outside their classrooms, high school department chairs can reduce some of the tension between their work as teachers in the classroom and their work as teacher leaders outside the classroom. Administrative support can help this effort to succeed. The following case study from Shiloh High School, Snellville, Georgia, illustrates how one school supported the efforts of veteran teachers to become leaders, without the need for formal leadership positions.

TALENT

TALENT (Teachers as Leaders: Encouraging New Thought) began in 2001 as an opportunity for veteran teachers with 15 or more years of experience who wanted to assume a greater leadership role within the school, but who did not want to be administrators or department heads—traditional school leadership positions. TALENT emerged from a need to provide a means for teachers to refine their leadership skills because for many, aside from continuing in graduate school, or moving out of the classroom, opportunities for teacher leadership are limited. Dr. Lea Arnau, who founded the TALENT program, explains that her goal as a staff developer is for teachers to self-direct their own professional growth.

The program philosophy rests on the premise that veteran teachers want to continue to grow and to learn, but in ways that acknowledge their experience, expertise, and interests. The TALENT program promotes *individualized* learning opportunities that the veteran teachers develop. Self-directed and self-initiated learning opportunities foster leadership. Learning is self-directed and self-initiated in that individuals choose a project with a leadership component, and then they are provided the opportunity for shadowing a chosen leader for one or more days, depending on the scope of the project. Topical seminars related to leadership and the lessons learned from shadowing administrators provide the structure for generating the seminar topics.

Teacher projects for TALENT include:

- Training of Mentors
- Development of Teacher Advisement Groups (Connect Groups)
- Participation in the development of state end-of-course exams
- Periodic review, summarizing, and sharing of educational law with faculty via e-mail
- Periodic review, summarizing, and sharing of special education journal articles with faculty via e-mail
- Development and delivery of system-wide staff development on reading strategies

In its inaugural year, seven teachers elected to participate in the program. During the first meeting, the vision for TALENT as a structure to promote self-initiated learning became the focus, and the participants developed and designed the program. The intent of the program was for the veteran teachers to discuss their theories about leadership and to initiate and complete a project that was meaningful to them and that included a leadership component. At subsequent meetings, the participants designed the format of the program—they took the lead in their own learning.

Dr. James Kahrs, Shiloh High School principal, supported the program by providing substitute days so the participants could shadow an administrator. In addition, Dr. Kahrs paid for TALENT T-shirts which were given to all participants as a means of advertising the program to others while affirming the veteran teachers' own involvement with the leadership program. Across the county, and within the state, people provided support and assistance by agreeing to be shadowed and interviewed by the TALENT participants—they gave of their time to share insights about leadership and learning.

Empowering teachers to become leaders is a process. Teachers will not automatically begin to think of themselves as leaders, particularly when their role within the school has not changed. The discussion that occurs at the TALENT meetings raises the awareness of the participants to leadership opportunities within the school and beyond.

What Does Teacher Leadership Mean for TALENT Teachers?

Teacher leadership is as individual as is each teacher. Leadership for one teacher might be speaking up at a department meeting on an issue that is important to her. Leadership for another teacher might be presenting at a national conference and sharing that presentation with faculty from his own school, while asking for committee volunteers to develop and implement his program. Every teacher has an area of interest or an area in which she wants to grow and, perhaps, develop expertise. As those skills are mastered, that teacher serves as a model to other teachers, thereby promoting teacher leadership.

Chapter Summary

The diversity of tasks teacher leaders have available to themselves in high schools is exciting: publicizing accomplishments, facilitating communication between department members and administrators, and supporting teachers' efforts to improve instruction. In addition, the more ordinary tasks of purchasing supplies and maintaining equipment also need to be done. Descriptions of these tasks can be found in the department chair's job description or the site's faculty handbook. Perhaps the greatest challenge for potential high school teacher leaders is to learn to manage the needs of the classroom and the responsibilities of being a teacher leader at the same time. A variety of skills is necessary to make this happen.

Where do teacher leaders learn the skills necessary to be leaders? One venue for this learning is at the site—on the job. Learning to be a teacher leader is ongoing, and teachers need to learn some skills to help them emerge as leaders. Schools and school districts need to provide professional development that supports the emergence of teacher leaders. The final chapter of this book addresses this need.

References

Delpo, A. M. (2001). Job interviews: Stay out of legal trouble. Retrieved November 28, 2001 from http://www.nolo.com/encyclopedia/article/emp/Inquiries.html

Siskin, L. S. (1991). Departments as different worlds: Subject subcultures in secondary schools. *Educational Administration Quarterly, 27*(2), 134–160.

Stevens, G. E. (1981). Taking the chance out of selection interviewing. *Journal of College Placement, 41*(2), 44–48.

6

Casting a Wide Net for Teacher Leadership

In this Chapter
- Scanning the Environment for Teacher Leadership
- Teacher Leadership Is Invitational
- An Extended Case Study—Achieving the Impossible Dream

A Call for Increased Leadership

The premise of this book is that teachers can and should be leaders in their schools and systems without necessarily having to opt out of the classroom full-time. The arrangement of this book might suggest the opposite because we cast the work of teacher leaders in the roles that they assume—lead teacher, instructional coordinator, department chair. This arrangement was a tough call for us to make because we had to balance the work of teacher leaders not only in the roles they assume but also in a lexicon that everyone understands. The lexicon of teacher leadership includes so many different titles—Early Childhood Intervention Specialist, Title I Coach, Staff Development Representative, Grade Level Leader, At-Risk Coordinator, Technology Coordinator—that it is no wonder that the construct of teacher leadership is not as widely researched as one would think (and hope, too).

We conclude this book with an invitation for teachers to help scan the environment for opportunities to multiply leadership and to make teacher leadership a viable option to all teachers who comprise the learning community. An extended case study of the work of a school system committed to teacher leadership concludes our book.

Scanning the Environment for Teacher Leadership Opportunities

Schools will survive with existing leadership, but schools, if they are to flourish, need the leadership of teachers. The stakes are high for schools that do not embrace teacher leadership, and Barth (2001) asserts, "Indeed, if schools are going to become places in which all children are learning, all teachers *must* lead" (p. 444, emphasis in the original). Teacher leadership positively correlates to student learning. Barth reports a "powerful relationship exists between learning and leading," and that "only when teachers learn will their students learn" (p. 445). Teacher leaders promote learning when they lead, and this is why teacher leaders and others must find opportunities for teachers to be involved in leadership opportunities within the school and beyond.

The work of schools is immense, and this work cannot be accomplished through the efforts of merely the principal and other administrators at the site. Leadership and the opportunities to lead must be diffused to the single most important resource of the school—teachers. Diffusing leadership can only start in the principal's office—the challenges of diffusing leadership rest with teachers. Teachers need to seize opportunities to lead, to have their voices heard, and to make the critical decisions related to learning for both the students and the adults who comprise the school. We agree with Lieberman and Miller's assessment that teacher "leadership is iterative" (1999, p. 22). It is the iterative nature of leadership that teacher leaders must look to embrace and to multiply exponentially in their work in schools.

The reality is that not all teachers want to lead; some teachers are content to "do the job assigned" to them and little more. However, we believe that given the *opportunity, support*, and *affirmation*, most, if not all, teachers want to be leaders beyond the confines of their classrooms. Teacher leaders find opportunities to be inclusive and encourage their colleagues to step up to the proverbial plate. Teacher leaders provide this type of encouragement by scanning the environment looking for opportunities for their colleagues to engage in leadership.

Identify Leadership Opportunities

Teacher leaders look for opportunities to tap into the expertise of their colleagues. Tapping into expertise is more than delegating a job to another colleague. Numerous committees comprised of teachers engage in school-wide efforts such as implementing a new aspect of instruction (e.g., moving to authentic assessment, implementing manipulatives), providing professional development to assist with the implementation plan, coordinating the evaluation and assessment of results associated with implementation, and reporting results to the school as a whole.

The teachers who serve on such committees do so because they have expertise, interest, and desire to see gains in student achievement and school improvement. To have one teacher leader take charge of all the work and activities involved in implementing a change, such as assisting a grade level to change to interdisciplinary units, is a waste of leadership potential. This type of innovation is of such magnitude that several teacher leaders would serve to better the cause. Teacher leaders actively diffuse leadership to all teachers.

As a teacher leader, one way to diffuse leadership opportunities is to take stock of which leadership opportunities are available for other teachers to assume. According to Barth (2001), teacher leadership is essential to the health of a school in ten areas:

1. choosing textbooks and instructional materials;
2. shaping the curriculum;
3. setting standards for student behavior;
4. deciding whether students are tracked into special classes;
5. designing staff development and in-service programs;
6. setting promotion and retention policies;
7. deciding school budgets;
8. evaluating teacher performance;
9. selecting new teachers; and
10. selecting new administrators. (p. 444)

Ways to begin tracking leadership opportunities include identifying:

- The work that currently is in progress
- The work that needs to begin
- When this work needs to begin
- Which teachers have interest and expertise in the work
- Who is in charge of this work

Teacher leaders are in a solid position to recommend to the administration the teachers that should be encouraged to join in the work of school improvement.

Cast a Wide Net

Teacher leaders and administrators promote leadership by "casting a wide net" that encompasses the entire school community. Encompassing the entire community in leadership activities such as shared decision making is essential, because the proverbial "schoolyard" has become a complex playing field.

Teacher leadership will only develop in a school where more players actively participate in the work needed to support the development of teacher leadership.

Leaders, regardless of title or position, who empower teachers actively, consistently, and authentically:

- Believe, from the beginning, that people have the potential and desire to succeed, and then support them.
- Build on a person's strengths.
- Provide feedback—encouragement, praise, and positive criticism—to help them grow.
- Build team spirit through retreats, cooperative efforts, and brainstorming sessions.
- Set high standards and praise the results; teachers will be proud of their organization.
- Remove obstacles to teachers' success by providing the necessary resources.
- Encourage teachers to take risks, to step out and try something new.
- Make work exciting with a relaxed, positive attitude.
- Let people see the results of their work praised.
- Listen carefully. (Baloche, 1998, pp. 239–249)

Leaders who empower others through these methods not only cast the net widely, but they also send a strong message—that leadership is invitational.

Teacher Leadership Is Invitational

Wong and Wong's (1998) major premise in their book, *The First Days of School*, is that learning is invitational. We take liberty here to assert that teacher leadership is invitational. If the goal is to create the opportunities for teachers—all teachers—to emerge as leaders, then certain workplace conditions need to be in place. The school system itself must support and nurture the development of the talents of teachers. Leadership is inclusive, not exclusive, and, as such, the charge for school systems is to:

- Create opportunities for more teachers to share their expertise.
- Develop an ethos of support and care to nurture teacher leadership through mentoring teachers through the process of evolving as leaders.

- Embed leadership as learning opportunities in the day-to-day work of teachers.

Provide Professional Development and Mentoring for Teacher Leaders

Teachers come to the profession with varying experiences and backgrounds, and they have the basic skills needed to organize instruction, assess learning, manage a room full of children, and communicate with children and parents. However, teacher leaders assume formal and informal leadership roles, and, as leaders, teachers need to exert different skills—skills that go beyond the day-to-day work of the classroom. For example, teachers interact with students daily; however, teacher leaders extend communication beyond the classroom, and they might need assistance in learning how to communicate differently, with other adults. Closely related to communication are group-processing skills—reaching consensus, conflict resolution—and using these skills with adults is greatly different from using them with children.

Given these needs, teacher leaders can benefit from professional development aimed at enhancing leadership and the myriad skills that make good leaders better leaders. Professional development can include, for example, opportunities to:

- Shadow other teacher leaders over sustained time.
- Attend professional meetings, conferences, and workshops.
- Enroll in graduate school coursework in leadership.
- Get on a list-serve of teacher leaders and engage in the talk of leadership with peers.
- Read professional journals, participate in professional reading and discussion groups, or join a group interested in solving a school-wide problem.

Teacher leaders need opportunities for learning how to further leadership skills, and mentoring and induction to the culture of leadership is a prerequisite to supporting the new teacher leader. Teachers who are already leaders can assist by mentoring and inducting other teachers into new leadership roles. Like beginning teachers, teacher leaders new to a position or role need assistance as they learn the work of teacher leadership. Teacher leaders can act as a sounding board for new teacher leaders.

Assuming Leadership Can Be
Risky Business for the Newcomer to Leadership

Teachers who are risk takers, according to Stone (1995), "experience the freedom to take risks, which is important for growth and change" and, furthermore, "empowerment enlightens the teacher to the positive side of failure—learning what does not work and then trying again to find out what does" (p. 295). For teacher leaders to take risks, they need the support and encouragement from teacher leaders who have traveled an often lonely road. Teacher leaders can experience the positive side of failure—growth and development from the insights gained through taking the risk needed to succeed.

New leaders need time to learn the work of teacher leadership, and they need guidance and support as they exert leadership. Time is well spent engaging the new teacher leader in the "talk of leadership," leading the newcomer to make sense of her work. Making sense of experience includes not only talk (over an extended period of time) but also multiple opportunities to reflect on the meaning of work. Dialogue, reflection, and a return to experience will assist the new teacher leader to make significant contributions to her work as a leader. Learning the ropes takes time, and, during this time, the newcomer needs to be reassured of her work.

An Extended Case Study from the Field— Gwinnett County Public Schools, Georgia

---

Teachers as Leaders, Inc.

*Dr. Gale Hulme, Program Director
Georgia's Leadership Institute for
School Improvement
866 W. Peachtree Street, NW
Atlanta, GA 30308
(404) 385-4088 Fax: (404) 894-9675
Online: gale.hulme@galeaders.org

Yvonne Frey
Principal, Head Elementary School
1801 Hewatt Rd.
Lilburn, GA 30047
(770) 972-8050 Fax: (770) 736-4498
Online: www.headelementary.org
Gwinnett County Public Schools
Mr. J. Alvin Wilbanks, Superintendent

Dr. Patty Heitmuller
Principal, Harbins Elementary School
3550 New Hope Road
Dacula, GA 30019
(770) 682-4270 Fax: (770) 682-4285
Online: harbins.home.mindspring.com
Gwinnett County Public Schools
Mr. J. Alvin Wilbanks, Superintendent

Vivian Stranahan
Principal, Shiloh Elementary School
2400 Ross Road
Snellville, GA 30039
(770) 985-6883 Fax: (770) 736-2061
Online: www.gwinnett.k12.ga.us/ShilohES
Gwinnett County Public Schools
Mr. J. Alvin Wilbanks, Superintendent

*Dr. Hulme is the immediate past Executive Director of Professional Development for Gwinnett County Public Schools.

Philosophy of Teacher Leadership

Imagine what a school system can achieve by "casting a wide net" across an entire district—elementary, middle, and high schools. The Gwinnett County Public Schools (Georgia) takes teacher leadership seriously and in the 1980s an initiative, Teachers as Leaders, Inc. (TAL), emerged as a model to empower teachers across the entire school system. This was no small feat because in 2002, Gwinnett County Public Schools was the largest school district in Georgia and the 22nd largest school district in the nation. With more than 122,000 students, the district grows by 6,300 students per year. According to Dr. Gale Hulme, the former Executive Director, Professional Development of the Gwinnett County Public Schools, the system anticipates hiring 1,400 new teachers and adding eight new schools in the upcoming school year. Additionally, 20 new schools will be built over the next five years (2002–2007). Hulme indicates:

> Gwinnett schools are large and complex and becoming more diverse each year. As a standards-based district focuses on continuous quality improvement, Teachers as Leaders, Inc. is one more way to ensure that a cadre of teacher leaders is ready to meet the diverse needs of students and to provide higher levels of learning for all students.

This is the philosophy of teacher leadership in the Gwinnett County school system.

The following case study is worth reading carefully, perhaps even several times. This case illustrates best practices about how teacher leadership emerges not as a mere program, but as an integral part of learning for teachers and site- and district-level administrators and how this learning positively affects the school community by casting a wide net that captures possibilities.

Teachers as Leaders, Inc. (TAL)

TAL is a leadership development program for educators designed to empower educators to use leadership skills to strengthen teaching and learning within a community that is constantly changing. The program structure is much like the Chamber of Commerce leadership development programs. Every year, a class of 30 to 35 educators participates in a fall retreat, three daylong programs, monthly study groups, a spring retreat, and various other learning opportunities. TAL alumni form as an alumni association and participate in learning and leadership opportunities both within their schools and throughout the Gwinnett County Public Schools.

> The vision of Gwinnett County Public Schools is to become a system of world-class schools. The vision includes schools that offer high academic standards for all students; accurate assessments to measure what students know and can do; a challenging curriculum; a safe, orderly learning environment; instructional strategies that address the differences in learning styles among students; accountability tools that measure a school's and the system's performance; and competent and inspired teachers and leaders. This tall order can be achieved only through leadership—leadership in the classroom, as well as leadership in the administrative ranks.
>
> **Dr. Gale Hulme, Program Director**
> **Georgia's Leadership Institute for School Improvement**

Early Beginnings of TAL

For the decade of the 1980s, Gwinnett County Public Schools (GCPS) was led by a superintendent committed to transitioning the school system from an organization serving a small rural population to one responding to the needs and expectations of a diverse suburban community experiencing rapid growth. To achieve that transformation, then superintendent Dr. Alton C. Crews emphasized district-level accountability, site-based decision making, and leadership development. Developing principals as instructional leaders capable of moving their schools and communities toward educational excellence was the focus of leadership development in the district.

In 1990, a new superintendent initiated a broad-based strategic planning process involving staff, parents, students, and community members to set the district's direction in light of new challenges and opportunities.

> Teachers must see themselves and their roles very differently. Instead of being primarily dispensers of information, teachers must reinvent themselves as leaders capable of engaging students in personalized learning experiences.
>
> **George Thompson**
> **Former Superintendent, Gwinnett County Public Schools**

George Thompson increased shared decision making by intentionally engaging teachers as leaders and encouraging significant partnerships in collaborative efforts both at the district and school levels. Because teachers have been historically isolated from each other and have not intuitively seen themselves as leaders, Thompson widened the district's commitment to leadership to include a specific initiative targeting teacher leadership. That initiative became

Teachers as Leaders, Inc., or TAL. Today, TAL continues as a nonprofit corporation serving the Gwinnett County schools. A Board of Trustees comprised of teachers, community leaders, and Gwinnett County Public School's administrators, in collaboration with an Executive Board, governs TAL.

Thompson charged the district's staff development department with developing the program. Because he valued collaboration, Thompson employed the services of an independent consultant who had extensive experience in creating programs of this nature. The staff development department and the consultant convened a group of educators and community representatives to serve as the first Board of Trustees. The Board divided into a number of implementation committees to design the various program components and to raise funds to support TAL's efforts. Thompson's vision of teacher leadership served as the starting point for developing the program's goals. Early in its history, the original TAL incorporated as a nonprofit organization, and the original Board of Trustees developed goals. The Board of Trustees has continued to revise program goals as needed to meet participant and district needs. Because TAL was under a tight time line to select the first class and begin the program experience, *the Board essentially built the plane as they were flying it.*

TAL Today

Today, under the administration of Superintendent Alvin Wilbanks, Teachers as Leaders Inc. continues to be a viable avenue for the development of teacher leaders.

> The mission of Gwinnett County Public Schools is to pursue excellence in academic knowledge, skills and behavior for each student, resulting in measured improvement against local, national, and world-class standards. Ensuring that all students learn at high levels requires creating a context for all teachers to learn at high levels as well. TAL extends professional learning opportunities for teachers to develop their leadership capacity to create the conditions for enriched learning for all students.
>
> **Alvin Wilbanks**
> **Superintendent, Gwinnett County Public Schools**

A Board of Trustees governs TAL. The Board is comprised of elected teachers, business leaders, administrators, and community members who serve on a three-year, rotating basis. The purpose of the Board is to maintain the integrity of the program, conduct long-range planning, and ensure the financial growth of the organization.

The steering committee, made up of TAL alumni serving as committee chairpersons, oversees the daily operations of the program. Chairpersons serve in a chair, vice-chair rotation. They lead committees of TAL alumni and community members to plan retreats, day programs, study groups, selection, and the alumni association.

The Philosophy of TAL

Teachers as Leaders, Inc. operates on the philosophy that teachers are an untapped resource for leadership within the classroom, school, system, and community-at-large. TAL empowers teachers by enabling them to have a wide-angle view of the community and the forces that drive decisions. TAL develops and affirms the concept of teacher as leader. TAL rests on the premise that teachers can contribute in significant ways to the larger community and can serve as leaders within their own schools as well.

> The focus of experiences is to break down the isolation of the classroom so that teachers broaden their appreciation for the community, the resources available in the community, and the commitment needed in the individual pursuit of excellence.
>
> Through various programs, TAL creates networking possibilities that empower teachers to develop their leadership abilities. TAL helps teachers see "the big picture" of community issues that impact student success.
>
> **Yvonne Frey**
> **Principal, Head Elementary School, Gwinnett County Public Schools**

The Goals of TAL

The long-range goal of the TAL program is to enhance student learning through teacher leadership. However, there are intermediate and immediate goals that TAL strives to achieve and include. These are set out in Figure 6.1.

The Leadership Curriculum of TAL

Each program includes specific goals designed to inform and strengthen teachers' leadership skills. During the *Fall Retreat*, teachers examine their own personality preferences as a means of making decisions, promoting personal development, and understanding, communicating, and teaming with others. They participate in team-building initiatives to strengthen group and analysis skills. They learn about the history of Gwinnett County and about national and state issues that affect local decisions.

Four one-day programs follow the Fall Retreat. The first examines the factors that influence growth in the community. Teachers hear firsthand from business and community leaders, city planners, and elected officials about the positive and negative aspects of growth on business, schools, and community.

Figure 6.1. Goals of Teacher as Leaders, Inc.

Ultimate	♦ To enhance student learning through teacher leadership
Intermediate	♦ To raise the status of an appreciation for the role of teachers. ♦ To increase professionalism, pride, vision, and confidence among teachers. ♦ To offer opportunities for leadership.
Immediate	♦ To affirm teachers. ♦ To encourage continuous improvement. ♦ To develop greater awareness of customers' needs. ♦ To provide a quality Teachers as Leaders program for Gwinnett County Public Schools' teachers. ♦ To promote dialogue about leadership among teachers, principals, and the community.

The second program, *Community at Risk*, focuses on the social, physical, mental health, and legal factors that impact at-risk students and their families. This day program is housed at the Gwinnett Detention Center, and includes a tour of both the Youth and Adult detention facilities.

The goals of *Education through the Eyes of the Region* day program include exploring Gwinnett's role in the metro Atlanta educational community, reframing the image of public education, and examining issues and challenges to the metro Atlanta educational community. A highlight of this program is a conversation with school superintendents representing the metro Atlanta school systems.

The final day program focuses on the Gwinnett County Public School System as the *Hub of the Community*. Each presenter focuses on the legacies of leaders within the school system, and the important contributions each has made on the direction of the county. Teachers examine the technical education, special education support services, and alternative school opportunities available to students in the system. The Hub program also explores the vision of the future of the school system.

TAL participants are provided the opportunity to visit the state legislature while it is in session, are given an audience with several key leaders to discuss legislative issues that impact education in Georgia, and participate in *study groups*. The groups meet after each retreat and day program. This time is used to reflect on the programs and determine ways to use what is learned to inform teaching and learning. Study groups also participate in a book study.

Finally, TAL participants conduct a *community service initiative* with members of their study group. Examples of past involvement include working on a Habitat for Humanity home project, collecting books for the Youth Detention Center, and volunteering at a women's emergency shelter.

Program Evaluation

Program evaluation is ongoing to ensure continuity and quality. When planning for class participants, careful consideration is given to session evaluations. The program continues to evolve based on reflections of participants, key education issues, the changing demographics of the community, and future trends in the region. One example of a modification is the addition of *Education through the Eyes of the Region Day*. As the metro Atlanta area changes, many school systems face new challenges. The need for a wider perspective and a common understanding became the catalyst for this program's development.

At the administrative level, the Board of Trustees, steering committee, and planning committee structures have gone through review and adjustments over time to meet the changing needs of the organization. The involvement of community leaders and alumni representatives in key leadership roles, and the use of a staggered rotation enable the Teachers as Leaders program to continue to evolve and strengthen over time.

> The Teachers as Leaders program exists to inspire teachers to seek innovative approaches to teacher leadership challenges, and to ultimately prepare students to meet the challenges of the larger community. With the involvement of Teachers as Leaders alumni, the program continues to grow and change to meet our fast-paced and ever changing world.
>
> **Dr. Patricia Heitmuller, Principal**
> **Harbins Elementary School, Gwinnett County Public Schools**

Lessons Learned

TAL has learned that many teachers want to become better leaders in their classrooms, in their schools, and in the community. Further, the program has proven that leadership can be taught. Given the opportunity, many teachers will step up to the leadership challenge and make significant contributions. Through opportunities to interact with peers and with other experts, teachers report a fuller understanding and appreciation of themselves as leaders.

The support of the school principal, both during the first year of involvement and in encouraging leadership opportunities in the future, is integral to the long-range success of the program. Therefore, the application process has been modified to provide a stronger emphasis on principal endorsement.

The challenge for TAL planners is to continue to provide time for meaningful discussions. These guided sessions enable teachers to reflect on innovative ways to transfer information about the initiatives, which will ultimately enhance student learning and productive citizenry. Time is an equal-opportunity factor. Everyone has the same amount of time. The question was not, "Do we have the time to develop teacher leaders," rather, it became, "How do we carve out the time needed for teachers to develop their leadership capacity?" In the business world, people are often provided time to grow professionally on-the-job, as part of their job. Continuous learning is an expectation to meet the changing conditions and rising expectations of a challenging world.

Funding TAL

When TAL began, a substantial amount of money was collected from the business community. These initial donations were used to form a TAL endowment account with the Gwinnett Community Foundation. The goal is to continue to add contributions to this foundation, eventually accumulating enough money for the TAL program to operate solely from the interest on the endowment. Community leaders interested in promoting professionalism and leadership of teachers in education assist with fundraising. Throughout the years, the Gwinnett County Board of Education has supported the program through the funding of release days for teachers, as well as materials for study groups and leadership assessment instruments.

Local school principals have also been supportive of TAL, not only through fiscal donations, but also by giving teachers release time to participate. Although it does not cover the cost of the program, participants pay a $400.00 tuition fee. At the successful conclusion of the program, teachers receive a professional development stipend of $300.00. Tuition fees combined with principals' contributions help to meet the program budget. Program funding also comes from the alumni of the organization.

Networking

One of the goals of TAL is to promote networking among teacher participants with their Gwinnett County Public Schools' colleagues, as well as networking between teachers and the business community. Business/Community members serve on the Board of Trustees and help to plan and organize TAL events. Business leaders also sponsor program days by providing breakfast, lunch, and snacks for class participants. TAL is listed on the Gwinnett County Chamber web site as one of Gwinnett's prominent leadership programs.

Program days lend themselves easily to networking through guest speakers and panel discussions geared to the topic or focus of the day. For example, *Education through the Eyes of the Region Day* includes not only public schools, but also representatives from private, parochial and home school sectors. The *Community at Risk* program includes guest speakers and panel members from Health/Human Services, the Department of Family and Children's Services (DFACS),

Sheriff's Department, and Juvenile Court System. The purpose of the program days is to provide opportunities to expand the perspectives of teachers by meeting with community leaders and discussing specific topics, trends, challenges, and issues.

Benefits of TAL

Former Superintendent Alton Crews used to say that the classroom is "where the rubber meets the road." With TAL, Gwinnett County Public Schools invests in its teachers and in developing their leadership capacity to skillfully navigate the often divergent, sometimes bumpy, and often exciting roads leading to higher levels of student learning.

> Teachers as Leaders, Inc. benefits Gwinnett County Public Schools' needs by taking good teachers and helping them become leaders in the classroom and community. TAL taps the leadership potential residing in teachers and helps them collaborate with other outstanding professionals while developing networks of resources in the community and across schools. Moreover, teachers apply the leadership knowledge and skills acquired through TAL in their classrooms and in the larger community. Finally, teachers perceive that the TAL experience positively affects student achievement.
>
> **Vivian Stranahan, Principal**
> **Shiloh Elementary School, Gwinnett County Public Schools**

A perception survey was administered to TAL alumni in March 2002. One hundred seventy-six teacher leaders responded. Results indicate that teachers believe the TAL program has positively influenced their leadership knowledge and skills. Moreover, they believe that TAL has positively affected student learning. Of the 176 responding, 20 indicated they were serving in administrative ranks, whereas 151 were serving in the classroom ("no response" from five). This is a strong indication that the program is serving the audience intended—teachers who desire to enhance their leadership capabilities and remain in the classroom.

Data indicate that teachers are applying their leadership skills in their local schools. Of the 151 teachers in the classroom, 13 went on to serve as department chairs and 8 served as grade level chairs. Several of these teachers commented that they are more effective in these roles because of their TAL experience. Respondents indicate a wide range of other leadership roles assumed in their schools. Figure 6.2 lists the myriad ways in which TAL participants have assumed leadership.

Figure 6.2. Leadership Roles Assumed by TAL Participants

TAL participants assume leadership by:
- Applying for and facilitating after-school literacy grants
- Serving as chair of school mentor programs
- Assisting other teachers as mentors
- Working as Instructional Coordinators
- Assisting Student Council with community service
- Serving as Instructional Team Leaders
- Leading parent involvement workshops
- Beginning Junior Beta Clubs
- Orchestrating Holiday Hope campaigns
- Organizing, planning, and implementing staff development to address areas of student needs identified in school improvement processes

Teachers take the TAL experience and internalize it in different ways. Some return to their schools to become leaders and some become involved in curriculum and instructional issues and committees at the county level. Still others become leaders in their own communities. Some leadership programs have directly resulted from, or been modeled after, TAL. For example, Gwinnett County Public Schools now has a Gwinnett Student Leadership Team and several TAL programs in local schools. TAL alumni have initiated each of these programs.

Administrative Support Needed to Promote Teacher Leadership

Principals

Principals play a crucial role in nurturing the leadership potential of teachers. Serving as leaders of leaders, principals create the context for teacher growth by providing ongoing support for teacher learning. Nominating the teacher candidate is a first step. It communicates, "I believe in you and your potential." Beyond their nominator role, principals also serve as listeners, blocking out time to hear "how it is going" and to be supportive of the teacher's learning journey. Principals model the way for teachers by demonstrating how an instructional leader maintains a focus on student learning, in spite of the daily distractions of running a school. Along the way, principals serve as role models showing teachers how to balance the complexities of leadership with the realities of conducting one's life.

Once teachers have graduated from TAL, principals pave the way for teachers to exercise their newly found leadership within the school, by giving them opportunities to lead school initiatives, and across the district, by supporting their inclusion on various district-wide committees. As teachers approach their principals about leadership opportunities in the community, principals serve as encouragers and cheerleaders. Finding ways to recognize, nurture, and celebrate the teacher in leadership growth is an important role for principals.

At various times, the principal may serve as facilitator, mentor, coach, and broker of resources. Principals must strike a careful balance between pressure and support to help teachers realize their leadership potential. Without a doubt, the principal's role as "leader of leaders" is critical to teacher growth and development. For this reason, TAL depends on principal nomination and support. In Gwinnett, principals have shown their commitment to TAL and advocacy for teacher empowerment by contributing financially to the program as well.

District Level

Gwinnett County Public Schools has enjoyed a rich legacy of superintendents and boards who have recognized the importance of leadership at all levels of the organization. Over time, this commitment has evolved. Current Superintendent Alvin Wilbanks defines our business as teaching and learning with an emphasis on learning. Wilbanks focuses clearly on achieving desired results through continuous quality improvement, and he has continued to support TAL.

One of the district's roles is to communicate the importance of leadership development. When Superintendent George Thompson introduced Teachers as Leaders, Inc., the first grant came from BellSouth Foundation. At that time, the executive director of BellSouth Foundation posed a question, "If teacher leadership is sufficiently important for you to request foundation dollars to support it, why has the school system invested no dollars in supporting it?" Superintendent Thompson responded that it would take outside funding and some initial success to help the school board and community understand the value of TAL. Former Superintendent George Thompson, who now serves as president of the Center for Leadership in School Reform, indicates that:

> I remain convinced that teaching is a leadership profession and that leaders are known by what they get others to do. I was not only looking to create a cadre of teacher leaders who would grow personally and professionally and who would provide support for one another. I was also looking for something symbolic that could create broader understanding of how isolated teachers can be as they work in cellu-

lar structures that discourage leadership and collaboration, and that result in low to moderate levels of staff engagement. I have never forgotten the question that Pat Willis, then executive director of the BellSouth Foundation, asked: "When I hear superintendents, boards, and principals complain about how hard it is to get teachers to take a leadership role, I ask, 'What percent of your budget does your district spend on the development of teachers as leaders?'"

The district professional development budget has supported TAL financially by providing for release days and by paying for participant leadership assessments and study group materials. This contribution, in conjunction with resources from the business community and principals, sustains TAL.

Even though TAL is a nonprofit corporation, it is important for the district to sanction the effort, and it is important for the district to provide a staff person to coordinate the TAL effort. It is important to have a point person to assist the Board of Trustees, to work closely with the Steering Committee, and to conduct ongoing evaluations of the program to ensure that it continues to meet system needs.

Community Level

TAL depends on leading business and community members, along with teachers and administrators, to serve on the Board of Trustees. As the governing board, the Board of Trustees maintains the integrity of the program and serves as the chief fundraising arm of the organization. These leaders serve as the "keeper of the vision." A Steering Committee, comprised of TAL alumni and community members, handles the day-to-day operation of TAL. Those who give their time freely communicate their support of teachers and their efforts to develop their leadership capacity. Business leaders and other community leaders frequently serve as program presenters and help keep teachers in touch with community issues. As part of community outreach, TAL has recently extended membership to include a representative teacher from neighboring Buford City Schools in Gwinnett

The Heart of Teacher Leadership

Teaching, by its nature, is a very isolating profession. Because "knowledge is power," Teachers as Leaders provides opportunities that allow teachers to expand their view beyond the four walls of their classrooms. As one participating teacher explains, "What an opportunity for us to step out of our 'narrow world' to broaden our scope and extend our own limited boundaries."

It is easy for teachers to go into their classrooms, close the door, and—alone—do the best they can. TAL effectively works to break down these walls of isolation. Another teacher participant notes,

> In planning curriculum presentations and involvement in the classroom, I have begun to consult business professionals, team members, and other colleagues to provide the most meaningful program for students. I have dared to give students more input into instructional activities, including cooperative planning and problem solving.

Participation in TAL does not make teachers leaders, but rather enhances leadership skills and instills in teachers the confidence in their ability to make a positive difference not only in their local schools, but also in the school district and in their own communities. The comment heard most often from teachers is, "Make the program available to more teachers." Participation in the program opens the eyes and hearts of teachers to see that community leaders value what they do and respect them as professionals. Al Hombroek, business leader and former Steering Committee co-chair, captures the conviction of business leaders: "In the education provided by world-class teachers lies the future of our democracy."

References

Baloche, L. A. (1998). *The cooperative classroom: Empowering learning.* Upper Saddle River, NJ: Prentice Hall.

Barth, R. S. (2001). Teacher leader. *Phi Delta Kappan* 82(6), 443–449.

Lieberman, A., & Miller, L. (1999). *Teachers—transforming their world and their work.* New York: Teachers College Press.

Stone, S. J. (1995). Teaching strategies: Empowering teachers, empowering children. *Childhood Education* 71(5), 294–295.

Wong, H. K., & Wong, R. T. (1998). *The first days of school.* Mountain View, CA: Harry K. Wong.

Subject and Author Index

A

Accountability 34, 37, 48, 62–63, 73, 101
Accreditation Committee 3, 13
Action Research 11, 18, 53
Action Streams 12–13
Acumen 8
Administrative Team 32, 68, 69
Administrators 1, 3–6, 7, 10–14, 16, 18, 24–27, 29, 33, 36, 38, 40, 44–45, 48, 51, 64, 99
Advanced Placement Program (Courses) 109
After School Child-care Coordinator 19
Age Discrimination in Employment Act of 1967 112
Agenda 29–30
Americans with Disabilities Act of 1990 112
Arkansas State Department of Education 57
Arnau, L. M. 115, 116
Arrington, D. 61, 63, 64, 65
Assessment 11, 50, 60
    Daily Assessment 50
    Teacher-driven Assessment 50
Assistant Principal 9, 15, 19, 34, 38, 57, 60, 63, 99
Assistant Superintendent 9
Associate Principal 99
Astuto, T. 16, 19
Authority 13, 15–16, 21, 38
    Formal Authority 15–16, 21
    Informal Authority 15–16
Autonomy 13, 27
Award Ceremonies 93

B

Bacon, F. 25
Baloche, L. A. 122, 136
Barnett, B. G. 16, 19
Barth, R. S. 120, 121, 136
Beltrani, L. 56–57
Bickert, T. S. 43, 55, 66
"Big Picture" View 4, 5, 11, 48
Blackwood, B. 56
Block Scheduling 102
Board of Education 37
Boles, K. 14, 15, 19
Bona Fide Occupational Qualification 112
Budget 23, 38, 39, 102–103
    Departmental Budget 23, 101, 102–103
    District Budget 38
    Grade Level Budget 23
Burnout 31

C

Cadre Persons 58–59
Call to Teacher Leadership 2, 9
Camp Turning Points 89–92
Capacity 2, 12, 65
Case-sensitive Information 26, 40
Central Office Administrators 4, 33, 51
Chain of Command 40
Change 2, 3, 12, 16, 27, 58
Change Agent 2
Character Questions 110–111
Chard, S. 56, 66
Career Continuum 7
Choir/Vocal Music 35, 53
Classroom Observations 26, 61, 63, 64
Climate 6, 24, 73
Coercive Power 22, 24
Cohagan, C. A. 61, 62, 64
Cohagan, R. W. 61
Collaboration 9, 27, 28, 31, 51, 77
Colleagues & Collegiality 6, 7, 10, 21, 24, 25, 27, 28, 31, 33
Committees 3, 13, 15, 33, 120–121
    Accreditation Committee 3

137

Committee Chair 17, 96
Curriculum (Development) Committee 3
School Improvement Committee (Team) 3
Search Committee 3
Selection Committee 15, 17
Communication 4, 11, 14, 16, 18, 28, 34, 40, 44, 51, 54, 57, 60, 63, 65, 113–114
Communication Patterns 4, 14
Communication that Asks 113
Communication that Evaluates 113–114
Communication that Helps Plan 113
Communication that Informs 113
Community 2, 3, 5, 6, 15, 19
Community of Teacher Leaders 16
Conference Presentations 15, 23, 43
Confidentiality Issues 28, 39, 61
Conflict 18, 21, 33, 34–38, 40
Conflict Resolution 18, 21
Connection Power 22, 23, 26–27, 93
Connections 26, 27
Context 4, 14
Counselors 34, 51, 60
Cross Disciplinary Planning and Themes 85, 87
Cross-grade-level Meetings 56
Culture 4, 24, 28, 30
Curriculum 3, 9, 11, 24, 31, 32, 35, 43, 48–53, 55
Curriculum Alignment 22, 48–53
District-wide Curriculum Alignment 48, 50
In-site Curriculum Alignment 50
Trans-site Curriculum Alignment 50
Curriculum Analysis 48–50
Curriculum Committee 3
Curriculum Development 18, 31
Curriculum Director 9
Curriculum Guides 101, 108–109
Curriculum Maps/Mapping 51
Curriculum Planning 85
Evaluating Curriculum 11
Exploratory Curriculum 85, 88, 93
Highly Aligned Curriculum 48–50
Overlapping Curricula 48–50
Real Curriculum 48–50
Spiral Curriculum 52
Tested Curriculum 48–50
Written Curriculum 48–50

Curriculum Development 18, 31
Curriculum Director 9
Curriculum Maps/Mapping 51

D

Data 26, 33, 55, 59, 81
Data Analysis 81
Data Collection 33, 55, 59–60
Decisions/Decision-making 2, 3, 9, 10, 12, 13, 18, 19, 21, 26, 38–41, 44, 55, 62
On-site Decision Making 9
Shared Decision Making 18, 62
Delpo, A. M. 111, 118
Demonstration Lessons 61, 72
Department 16, 23, 25, 27, 28, 29, 33, 48
Department Chair 1, 3, 16, 18, 21, 24, 32, 34, 35, 36, 37, 95, 96–118
Business Manager 97
Content Specialist 105
Curriculum Coordinator 97
Novice Department Chair 97, 102, 114
Public Relations Officer 97
DeQueen Primary School (DeQueen, AR) 54, 56–60
DeQueen Public Schools (DeQueen, AR) 56–60
Development, Adult Stages 5
Direct Instruction Coordinator 58–60
Direct Instruction Reading Initiative 57–60
Discrimination 112
Disciplinary Problems 26, 56
District 3, 32, 50, 52
Dodge, D. T. 43, 55, 66
Dunst, R. 15, 19
Duty 29, 54
Duty Periods 29
Duty Schedule 54
Dykes, S. 57

E

Earned Leadership 11
Educational Myopia 5
Empowerment 13–15, 25, 26, 27, 65
English (as a subject) 36–37
English, F. 48–49, 66
Environment 3, 10, 12, 29, 30, 47, 56
Learning Environment 3, 15, 47, 56
Equal Pay Act of 1963 112
Equipment 102, 103–104
Consumable Equipment 103
Expectations of Teacher Leaders 24

Subject and Author Index

Experienced Teachers (see Veteran Teachers)
Expert Power 22, 24–25
Expertise 4, 6, 7, 16, 25, 27, 31, 48, 76, 113, 120, 122
Exploratory Curriculum 85, 88, 93
Extrinsic Rewards 5

F

Facilities 99, 103
Faculty Handbooks 24, 97, 99
Faculty/Staff Meetings 7, 11, 62
First-year (Novice) Teacher 4, 7, 15, 30, 36, 44
Flexible Scheduling 70
Formal Authority 15–16, 21
Formal Leadership 8, 15, 16, 43, 60
French, J. R. 22, 41
Frey, Y. 124, 128
Fullan, M G. 27, 41

G

Gifted and Talented 54
Goals 10, 11, 30, 36, 50, 63, 79
Grade Level Chairs 96
Grade Level Leaders 16, 24, 32, 37, 53–57, 60, 72
Grade Level 12, 16, 23, 25, 27, 28, 29, 33, 51, 52, 53, 59, 62–65
Graduate School 15, 38
Grants 33, 57
Griffin-Spalding Public Schools (Griffin, GA) 69
Group Processing Skills 16, 18
Growth 4, 5, 6, 8, 11, 16, 19, 64
Gunter Elementary School (Gunter, TX) 60–65
Gunter Independent School District (Gunter, TX) 61
Gwinnett County Public Schools (GA) 10, 115, 124–136

H

Harbins Elementary School (Dacula, GA) 124, 130
Head Elementary School (Lilburn, GA) 124, 128
Heitmuller, P. 124, 130
Hersey, P. 23, 41
High School 1, 95–118
Hiring New Staff 65

Holloway, L. 73
Horejs, J. 53, 66
"How" of Teacher Leadership 1
Hulme, G. 124, 125, 126
Huse, E. F. 32, 41

I

Immigration Reform and Control Act of 1986 112
Inclusive Leadership 21
Induction 30–31, 54, 57
Influence 5, 7, 13, 16
Informal Authority 15–16
Informal Leadership 16, 40, 43
Informational Power 22, 23, 25–26
Inquiry 18, 19
Inservice 45
Instructional Coordinator 1, 3
Instructional Improvement 65
Instructional Lead Teacher 1, 17, 61, 67, 68, 79
Instructional Leadership 63–64
Insular Shortsightedness 5
Interdisciplinary Cooperation 82
Interdisciplinary Team Planning 86–87
Interviewing 101, 110–111
Interviewing Questions 110–111
    Character Questions 110–111
    Motivation Questions 110–111
    Pedagogical Questions 110–111
    Stress Questions 110–111
Intrinsic Rewards 5
Inventory 32, 103
Isolation 21, 26, 27, 29–31, 40, 82
Itinerant Teachers 35, 51

J

Jablon, J. R. 43, 55, 66
Jalongo, M. R. 13, 19
Jarboe, T. 73, 74, 75, 76, 77, 78
Job Descriptions 22, 24, 25, 54, 57, 58, 69, 97
    Department Chair 97
    Direct Instruction Coordinator 58
    Grade Level Leader 54
    Instructional Lead Teacher 69
    Smart Start Facilitators 57
Job Interviews 110
Junior High School 67

K

Kahn, R. L. 32, 41
Kahrs, J. R. 115, 116
Katz. D. 32, 41
Katz, L. 56, 66
Katzenmeyer, M. 16, 19
Kruglanski, A. W. 23, 41

L

Lambert 3, 19
Language Arts 70
Law/Legal Issues 37, 111–112
    Age Discrimination in Employment Act of 1967 112
    Americans with Disabilities Act of 1990 112
    Bona Fide Occupational Qualification 112
    Discrimination 112
    Equal Pay Act of 1963 112
    Federal Legislation and Accountability 112
    Immigration Reform and Control Act of 1986 112
    Interviewing 111–112
    Title VII, Civil Rights Act of 1964 112
Lead Teachers 1, 3, 16, 43
Leaderful Organizations 9
Leadership 1, 7–9, 11, 15, 21, 30, 40, 43, 119
    A.I.M. 7–9
    Acumen for 8
    Adeptness for 8
    Connection Leadership 93
    Earned 11
    Formal 8, 15, 16, 21, 43, 60
    Informal 15, 16, 21, 40, 43
    Interest in 8
    Motivation for 8
    Opportunities 120
    Underground Leadership 40
Leadership Plunge 12
Learning 6, 10, 15, 19, 27, 28, 29, 30, 37, 43, 44, 51, 53, 54–58, 61–63, 65
    Collaborative Learning 27
    Learning Capacity 65
    Learning Environment 3, 15, 56
    Learning String 53
    Learning Teams 58
    Lifelong Learning 43
    Student Learning 2, 23, 54, 55, 57, 62
    Styles of Learning 10, 51

    Teachers' Learning 29, 54, 58, 62, 63
Learning Community 27, 57
Legitimate Power 22, 24
Lesson Plans 26, 59
Lexicon of Leadership 119
Lieberman, A. 14, 19, 40, 41
Lifelong Learning 43
Lightfoot, S. L. 13, 19
Local School Council 19
Lomas, A. 53, 66
Lortie, D. C. 27, 41

M

Maintaining Equipment 102, 103–104
Managing Director 9
Mathematics 24, 34, 55, 70
Mayers, R. S. 49, 66
McQuaide, J. 83, 94
Media Specialist 60
Meditationes Sacrae 25
Meetings 7, 11, 54, 56, 105–108
    Agendas 106–107
    Conducting Meetings 105–108
    Cross-grade-level Meetings 56
    Faculty Meetings 7, 11
    Grade Level Meetings 54–56
Mentoring 3, 7, 11, 15, 43, 54, 57, 64, 70, 100, 123
Middle School 1, 67–94
    Middle School Philosophy 73, 82
Miller, L. 14, 40, 41, 120, 136
Mission 8
Moller, G. 16, 19
Money/Monetary Compensation 2, 6
Morale 3
Motivation 8–9, 100
Motivation Questions 110–111
Multidisciplinary Themes 87

N

Nettles, B. 89, 91
Newsletters 47
Networking 26, 70
Networks 51, 60
Norman Public Schools (Norman, OK) 80
Norms 28

O

Oklahoma National Guard 89–91
Omnidisciplinary Themes 87
Orchestra 53

Subject and Author Index

Oversight of Budgets 102–103

P

Pacing Guides 59
Paper Screening 110
Paraprofessionals 29, 51, 55
Parent–Teacher Conference 44–48
Parent–Teacher Organization 47
Parents 1, 3, 5, 6, 19, 31, 44–48, 51, 54, 82, 113
Patrons 113
Pedagogy 51
Pedagogical Questions 110–111
Peer Coach(ing) 3, 11, 17, 22, 23, 72, 82
Personnel 26, 38, 44
Plano Independent School District (Plano, TX) 52, 66
Policies 4, 23, 46
Polite, M. M. 87, 94
Politics 21, 28, 101
    Political Entanglements 101
    Political Tightropes 28, 33, 101
Positive Recognition Form 85–86
Power 21–27, 35, 38, 40, 65
    Coercive Power 22, 24
    Connection Power 22, 23, 26–27
    Expert Power 22,
    Informational Power 22, 23, 25–26
    Legitimate Power 22, 24
    Positional Power 22,
    Referent Power 22, 23, 25
    Reward Power 22, 25
Power of Personality 25
Powerless Leaders 22
Pre-school Retreat 30
Presentations 33
    Video Presentations 46
Presenters 3
Principal 9, 15, 19, 23, 34, 38, 39, 41, 57, 60, 61, 63, 64
Problem Posing Skills 18
Problem Solving Skills 16, 18
Professional or Staff Development 6–7, 10–11, 15, 17, 44–45, 51, 54, 55, 57–59, 62–65, 76, 82, 123
Program Evaluation 58–59, 63, 99

R

Raven, B. H. 22, 41
Record Book 26
Reference Groups 12–13
Referent Power 22, 23, 25
Reflection 18, 19, 58
Reflective Leaders 10
Regulations (State or Federal) 3–4,
Release Time 22, 23, 29, 32–33, 63
Renewal 5
Restructure Time 16
Reward Power 22, 25
Risk & Risk-taking 4, 7, 18, 27, 40, 56, 123–124
Role Ambiguity 21, 32–37, 40
Role Conflict 21, 32–37
Romanish, B. 13, 19
Runkel, P. J. 34, 41

S

Sagor, R. 16, 19
Schedules 3
Schmuck, R. A. 34, 41
School Improvement 2, 4, 16, 121
School Improvement Team 3, 18
School-wide Issues 16
Science 30, 55
Search Committee 3
Southwest Educational Development Laboratory (SEDL) 2, 19
Selection Committee 15
Self-evaluation of Curricular Units 51
Seminars 8, 51, 53
Shared Decision-making 18
Shared Governance 38–39, 74–75
Shared Vision 4
Shiloh High School (Snellville, GA) 115–116
Shiloh Elementary School (Snellville, GA) 124, 132
Siano, J. 89
Siskin, L. S. 96, 118
Smart Start 57–58
Social Studies 70
Spiral Curriculum 52–53
Standardized Tests 26, 60
Standards 10
State Departments of Education 9
State-mandated Tests 50
Stevens, G. E. 110, 118
Stranahan, V. 124, 132
Stress 30, 31, 32
Stress Questions 110–111
Stone, M. 53, 66
Student Learning 2, 23, 54, 55, 57, 62
Student Placement 59, 101, 109

Students 5, 6, 7, 11, 19, 32, 51, 59, 62, 76, 101, 109
    Achievement 76
    Student Growth and Development 5
    Student Placement 59, 101, 109
Subject Area Coordinator 18
Substitute Teachers 29
Superintendent 9
Supervising Instruction/Supervision 22, 53, 61
Supervisors 32, 35

T

Teacher Aides 55, 62
Teacher Evaluation 26, 37, 58
Teacher Facilitator 43, 60–65
Teacher Leaders and
    Authority 13, 15–16
    Cadre Persons 58–59
    Club Sponsors 18
    Committee Chairs 17
    Department Chairs 1, 3, 16, 17, 21, 24, 31, 35, 36, 37
    Direct Instruction Coordinators 58–60
    Grade Level Leaders 16, 18, 24, 31, 36, 37, 53–57
    Instructional Coordinator 1, 3
    Instructional Lead Teachers 1, 17, 61
    Iterative Nature 14, 40
    Lead Teachers 1, 3, 16, 21, 43
    Powerless Leaders 24
    Readiness for 6
    Reflective 10
    Subject Area Coordinators 18
    Risk-takers 4, 7
    Self-directed Nature 6
    Teacher Facilitators 43, 60–65
    Team Leaders 3, 32, 36, 83–86, 93
    Trust–builders 28
Teachers 5, 10, 11, 14, 19
    Content Specialists 105
    First–year (Novice) Teachers 4, 7, 30, 36, 44
    Itinerant Teachers 35, 51
    Substitute Teachers 29
    Veteran Teachers 4, 7, 30, 36, 44
Teachers As Leaders, Inc. (TAL, Inc.) 10, 119–136
Teachers' Learning 29, 54, 58, 62–63
Teaching Assignments 33, 53
Team 23, 25, 27, 28, 29, 33, 35, 52, 53, 62
Team Leader 3, 32, 83–86, 93

Survey 71
Team Meetings 84–85
Team Planning 62, 83
Technology 55
Tension 2, 27, 28, 31, 33, 61, 114
    Administrator–teacher Tension 31, 114
Test Scores 26, 46
Textbook Adoption 15, 50, 54
Thorny Issues 21–41
Time 3, 16, 22, 23, 29, 30, 32–33, 34, 35, 63
    Release Time 22, 23, 29, 32–33, 63
    Restructure Time 16
Title VII, Civil Rights Act of 1964 114
Transitions 88–92
    Elementary School to Middle School 88–92
    Middle School to High School 92
Troen, V. 14, 15, 19
Trust 11, 12, 24, 28, 29, 30, 31, 40, 61
Trust-building 28, 31, 40

U

UCLA School Management Program 9, 19
Underground Leadership 40

V

Variables (Context) 14
Vertical Alignment 51–53, 55
Vertical Articulation 108
Veteran Teachers 4, 7, 30, 36, 44
Video Presentations 46
Vision 4, 5
Voice 13–15, 52
Volunteers 47, 113

W

"When" of Teacher Leadership 1, 6–10,
Whittier Middle School (Norman, OK) 89–92 (see also Camp Turning Points)
"Why" of Teacher Leadership 1, 3, 5–6, 9
Wilbanks, J. A. 115
Wong, H. K. 122, 136
Wong, R. T. 122, 136
Woolfolk, A. E. 55, 66
Workshops 3, 8, 53
W. R. Coile Middle School (Athens, GA) 73–79

Z

Zepeda, S. J. 49, 66